To DR. KATHY

From Chopper

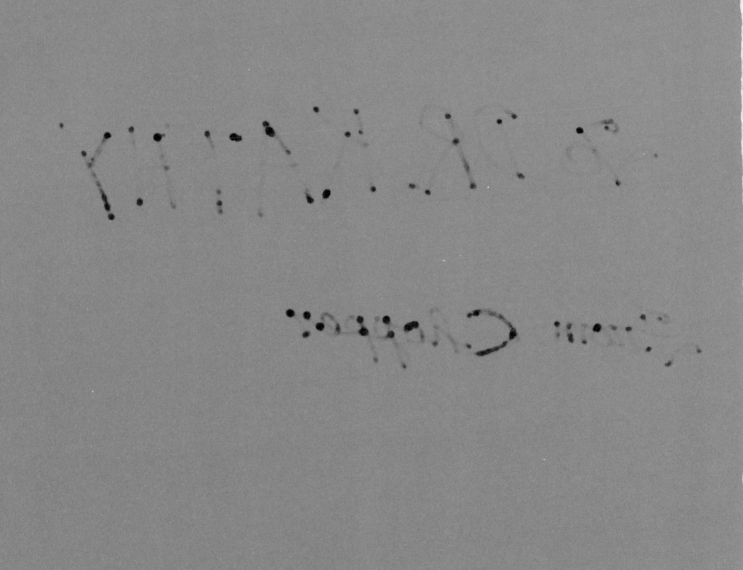

THE
French Bulldog

Kennel Club Books
A Division of BowTie, Inc.

EDITORIAL

Andrew DePrisco *Editor-in-Chief*

Peter Bauer *Managing Editor*

Amy Deputato *Senior Editor*

Jonathan Nigro *Editor*

Matt Strubel *Assistant Editor*

ART

Sherise Buhagiar *Senior Graphic Artist*

Bill Jonas *Book Design*

Joanne Muzyka *Digital Art*

The French Bulldog

Copyright © 2007

Kennel Club Books®
A Division of BowTie, Inc.

40 Broad Street • Freehold, NJ • 07728 • USA

Library of Congress Cataloging-in-Publication Data

Lee, Muriel P.
  The French bulldog / by Muriel P. Lee.
      p. cm. — (Kennel club classic series)
  Includes index.
  ISBN-13: 978-1-59378-680-9
  ISBN-10: 1-59378-680-8
  1. French bulldog. I. Title.
SF429.F8L4392 2007
636.72--dc22
                        2007011699

Printed and bound in Singapore

10 9 8 7 6 5 4 3 2 1

THE
French Bulldog

By Muriel P. Lee

Acknowledgments

The publisher would like to thank the owners of the dogs featured in this book, including:

Sande Abernathy
Teresa Bjork
Lucy Bonsal
Laura Bostwick
Mme. Bourquin
Marilyn Burdick
Mark and Beth Carr
Bob and Laura Condon
Donna Cron
James Dalton
Liz Davidson
Dorit Fischler
Graham Godfrey
Jim and Jan Grebe
Brad Hagmayer
Warren and Debbi Houtz

Bette Weinstein Kaplan
Manda S. Kaplan
Diane Laratta
Muriel Lee
Heidi Lillie
Michael and Nancy Magill
Joseph A. Martin Jr.
Richard and Carol Meyer
Stan and Teddy Mileham
Alan and Judith Miller
Andrea Morden-Moore
Carlene Naughton
Kath Parlett
Dulcie Partridge
Constance Payne
Mary Phelps

Sandra Plotts
Penny Rankine-Parsons
Ron and Suzanne Readmond
Michael Rosser
Colette Secher
Claire Senecal
Luis and Patty Sosa
Philip Stemp
Deb Stevenson
Sarah Sweatt
Chris Thomas
Scott Tomassi
Dr. John Turjoman
Kathy Dannel Vitcak
Vivien Watkins
Jim and Shauna Woodruff

Photography

Sande Abernathy
Ashbey Photography
Abiy Assefa
Carol Beuchat
Blaser Photography
Booth Photography
Laura Bostwick
Steve Bull/Sirius Photography
James Dalton
Dorit Fischler
Four Seasons Photography
Isabelle Français
Brad Hagmayer
Henry Photography

Amy Johnson
Bill Kramer
Terry Lansburgh
Heidi Lillie
Mary Evans Picture Library
Lazaro Montano
Andrea Morden-Moore
Next Age Photography
David Sombach Photography
Luis and Patty Sosa
Scott Taras
Scott Tomassi
Paula Trainer/A Different Image
Tom Weigand/The Winning Image

Left to right: Ch. Shann's Goodtime In Hollywood, Ch. Shann's Goodtime Celeste, Ch. Shann's Pudgybull Primadonna and Ch. Shann's Pudgybull Houdini.

Contents

PART IV Frenchie Royals & Aristocrats

PART V Bat Ears Abroad!

PART VI The Priceless Frenchie: Art & *Objets d'Art*

APPENDICES

INDEX

To the
French Bulldog

The body shape of dogs like you,
No sculptor's tools can e'er enhance.
You, sprightly dog of brindled hue,
You, bulldog of beloved France.
Neat, natty, smart and quick are you;
Possess'd of pluck and power, too.

Your full-brained skull denotes no fear;
It's filled with fighting intellect;
Your bat-like, listening, ready ear
Has made you ever circumspect.
Yes, dogs have brains, as well as we;
And use them quite as frequently.

You, foundling, yours no misery;
Your daily life is never hard:
Companion in the nursery,
In boudoir and on boulevard.
You, women's pet, you, children's need;
You, Frenchmen's choice of bulldog breed!

Anon.

INTRODUCTION

My life in dogs began around the age of eight when my parents purchased a Wire Fox Terrier. We didn't know what a terrier was, especially one called "Wire Fox," but my parents had watched *The Thin Man* movies and wanted a dog that looked just like Asta, the canine star of the series. Our Susie was well-bred and my mother learned how to groom her reasonably well, so she looked more or less like a proper Wire Fox Terrier. We didn't know a thing about training a dog, so Susie just grew and, true to her heritage, remained a wild pup until about the age of 12, when she began to slow down. She lived to the age of 16, when her spirit was finally spent.

I didn't have another dog until I was in my mid-20s, when I responded to a newspaper ad about a sheepdog puppy. "Is this the dog with the hair over its eyes?" "No, this sheepdog looks like a little Collie. You're looking for an Old English Sheepdog." Thus my entry into the world of pure-bred dogs. Three Old English and lots of grooming, along with some health heartbreaks, led me back to my beginnings, the terriers. And that began 20 years in Scottish Terriers with many litters and many champions.

Eventually I went through five years with no dogs and a new carpet, but as the carpet began to look a bit tired I thought again about getting a dog. The breed that stayed in my mind was one that had been recommended to me by many old-timers in the dog game. "If you could have only one dog, what would it be?" "Oh, a French Bulldog…they are great." A French Bulldog? What a funny-looking breed! However, I made some inquiries, as I thought this just might be the breed for our household. And when the first Frenchie came to live with us, I thought, this is a strange breed!

Will Judy wrote in 1935, "One must learn to like the Frenchie just as he learns to like olives but once having learned to like the Frenchie, he will never cease to speak the praises of the breed." How true, and it turned out that the Frenchie was the dog for us. What a breed! Not only is he an easy keeper and below-the-knee in size but he is also fun, cute as can be, smart and full of personality!

Welcome to the French Bulldog! In this book you will find the Frenchie in his full glory. You will learn of the breed's history, its health and its standard. And, best of all, you will see fabulous photographs of the Frenchie doing what he does best—looking smart, handsome, pretty, cute, fun and well dressed. Of course, not to be left out, he can be a dedicated little worker, jumping over hurdles, retrieving dumbbells and even doing a day's work as a certified therapy dog. In addition to all of that, the French Bulldog has been a favorite of the art world over the past century; you will find pictured in this book fabulous photographs of great Frenchie artwork and unusual objets d'art.

What more could one want in a breed of dog?

PART I
LE BON VIVANT

Left to right: Rosie (Tansey's mom), Lila Mae, Tansey (Lila's mom) and Spruce (half-brother to Tansey).

1

The
IRRÉSISTIBLE
French Bulldog

The section of the breed standard that describes the French Bulldog's temperament reads as follows: "Well behaved, adaptable and comfortable companions with an affectionate nature and even disposition; generally active, alert and playful, but not unduly boisterous." One sentence sums up the character of the French Bulldog quite well. However, this little Frenchman is so much more!

Unlike the terriers, who enjoy having a job and often need to have one in order to live in a household without driving everyone nuts, a Frenchie can do a day's work—but he really doesn't feel that this is essential in the scheme of things. The sporting dogs love to romp around in the field whether it is raining or snowing, muddy or sunny. A Frenchie is not eager to get his feet wet and isn't thrilled to be out in the very cold weather. In the heat of summer his owner knows better than to take him for a brisk walk around the lake, as his nose and ears will turn red and he will have difficulty breathing. In fact, overheating can cause serious problems for him. He can surely run and likes a good time, but don't expect him to take a five-mile race with you, as he will wear down faster than any hound.

What the Frenchie is best at is being a companion, and this is what he was bred for. He loves his master and mistress and any children in the household. He will gladly share the sofa for an evening of television or, even better, share your bed at night. And like a true Frenchman, he loves to eat and particularly likes to eat well. Shrimp, oysters, caviar, a good cut of meat and green vegetables are all enjoyed, and a birthday cake is always appreciated. He would probably like a glass of red wine before dinner, but since he has no thumbs he would have difficulty in picking up the crystal-stemmed glass.

The French Bulldog

The Frenchie likes to play and he likes to giggle. Even though he barely has a tail, when he leans down on his front legs, with his fanny in the air and his eyes saying, "Let's play," you can see that little tail stub wagging. He likes lots of soft toys and he wants them all around the house. Place a toy box or basket in every room, fill it with teddy bears and other soft plush toys, and he will be in his element. He loves the squeakers but may lose interest in a toy once the squeak is gone. Teddy bears with eyes that can be taken out are lots of fun, but you must watch and see that those little pieces are not swallowed.

He knows when you are sick or injured and he will be most sympathetic. Have a hip replacement and within a few days you may find your Frenchie limping around, in sympathy for your surgery. If you are sick in bed with a bad cold, your Frenchie will be lying beside you. And if you are feeling sad and lonely he will be there, offering a comforting lick of your hand.

Above: Brindle buddies: Rare-Breed Ch. Oakleafs Taboo of Fabelhaft (Presa Canario) with Frenchie Am./Can. Ch. Robobull Fabelhaft Inferno.
Facing page, top: Tansey, taking the notion of "bat ears" to a new extreme.
Facing page, bottom: "Do you think anyone can see me?"

The Irrésistible French Bulldog

Above: Tansey spends some time relaxing and just "hanging out" at the park the day after completing her Rally Advanced title.
Facing page, top: Frenchie life is always a day at the beach.
Facing page, bottom: A Frenchie is a girl's best friend.

The French Bulldog

Although the Frenchie is a great companion, he also has other attributes. The French Bulldog has been seen to make an ideal dog for therapy work. He is intelligent and can understand a task when given to him. Frenchies like to participate in agility, rally and obedience work and although they may require a bit of patience, most will take to the work with intelligence and interest.

He doesn't like to be scolded and he does not take well to harsh punishment. His feelings will "be hurt" and your buddy will not be a happy camper. With his intelligence, you can usually get your point across to him without breaking down his spirit.

As early as 1916, James Watson wrote in *The Dog Book*, "The French bulldog has been quite a prominent feature in the toy section of American dogdom for the past 15 years and the best evidence of his being a good dog about the house is the way those who take up the breed stick to it. Fanciers of the boule-dogue are anything but butterflies but hold to their pets with a persistence that might well be copied by the men who disturb other breeds by getting out before they have hardly had time to settle in the fancy. Not quite so rompy and active as the Boston terrier, the boule-dogue is nevertheless as lively in his movements as any dog needs to be about the house, possessing some of the sedateness of the pug in his temperament and disposition. He possesses the advantage which all short coated dogs have, of being easily kept clean and fit for the house, requiring only good daily grooming to that end."

The International Encyclopedia of Dogs says, "The 'Frenchie' has many advantages. It is small enough to get out of the way but big enough to look after itself. It is normally peaceful but alert enough to warn of strangers. It is strong and robust, yet with a modest appetite. It is short-coated and therefore easily groomed."

As one can see, the French Bulldog is not the average dog. With his distinguishing bat ears, he is an intelligent, fun-loving companion. If you bring love to his table, he will return it to you ten fold.

Above: It's a bird...it's a plane...no, it's Ch. Bon Marv's EZ as Pied Jackpot!
Facing page, top: Jackpot! I'm the Boss of JustUs looks ready to take on the world.
Facing page, bottom: Who can resist Waldo's fabulous Frenchie face?

Pattée and Spanky in Gran'ma's stone martin furs.

The
ÉLÉGANT
Well-dressed Frenchie

By Heidi Lillie

Whether dressed in a stylish sweater, a Halloween costume or an antique badger-hair collar, a well-dressed Frenchie is a sight to behold!

What is it that makes French Bulldogs so enticingly dressable? Their wonderfully expressive faces become even more adorable when adorned with a hat, a feather boa or a pair of bee-like antennae. Their expressions seem almost human once they have a pair of designer glasses wrapped around them. Their bully chests seem to puff with pride when wearing the right sweater, collar or gown. In short, French Bulldogs love to be admired! So many Frenchie owners love the attention that their unique dogs command and, once accessorized, a Frenchie becomes even more extraordinary (as if that's possible!).

Frenchies also have the right temperament for playing dress-up. Most French Bulldogs enjoy playing the model, as this is a breed that loves to please. When Frenchies know they are looking good and are getting recognition, laughter and accolades from their people, they seem to revel in it. Many a French Bulldog has allowed his or her child to dress him up to have a "tea party." Vintage photos show Frenchies being costumed by children, and this amusing pastime continues to this day due to the patient and loving nature of the breed. (Please make sure to always supervise toddlers with your Frenchie, as they may inadvertently be too rough when they get carried away with the fun of dressing up their "fwenchie.") Frenchies are just the right size for dressing up as well. Not too small, not too large, they can carry off just about anything! And best of all, they let us do it, no questions asked.

The French Bulldog

Why do people love to dress up their Frenchies? Sometimes simply for sheer fun, as with Halloween costumes, or to show their love for their devoted dog by having him don a birthday hat or a new collar for a special occasion. Some people dress them as an extension of themselves by putting them in designer finery. If the owner has the latest Louis Vuitton handbag, then of course Fido must have a collar to match! Not to mention the coordinating leash and the dog carrier.

It's been well documented in photos, lithographs and illustrations over the past 200 years that a "badger" collar was once seen on every French Bulldog of distinction. This is a leather collar that is framed on either side with real badger hair that fans out in a halo around the dog's neck. It essentially frames the dog's head and sets off his beautiful visage. Perhaps it was a status symbol, but it was definitely a fashion statement. Occasionally you can still find an original "badger" collar at an antique shop or at auction—with a very high price tag, of course. You can also find nice reproductions. One thing is for certain: the "badger" collar was one of the definitive starting points as far as accessorizing your Frenchie went.

The most famous image of a Frenchie in a "badger" collar comes from the front cover of the Westminster catalog from 1897. A tiny brindle is

Above, left: Darla models her Hollywood starlet look.
Above, right: Rhinestone cowdog Ch. Fisher's Mon Reve of Starhaven.
Facing page, left: The "badger" collar has long been the accessory of choice for the fashionable Frenchie.
Facing page, right: A modern take on the traditional "badger" collar.

nestled in the arms of his fashionable owner. Tons of vintage postcards show Frenchies in the fancy collars, and many of the dogs are in the arms or on the lead of an actress or another equally famous person. Photos of Colette, the French novelist, show her with her Frenchies in "badger" collars as do drawings by Toulouse-Lautrec. Of course, the Steiff French Bulldog stuffed animals are always seen wearing them, and the original antique Frenchie "Growler" pull toys are shown sporting badger-hair collars.

If you've seen the *Dogville* "All Barkie" film shorts from the late 1920s and early 1930s, they've upped the ante by featuring dogs of many breeds dressed to the nines, acting in parodies of old Hollywood films. One of the main "starlets" was none other than a French Bulldog! Recognized for her fabulous and expressive flat-faced mug, she stole the show, along with most of the leading roles! Check the films out on the Turner

Classic Movies channel or at www.tcm.com; this is a hilarious and fascinating genre of films featuring a treasure trove of well-dressed dogs.

In the recent movie *Bringing Down the House*, starring Steve Martin and featuring the very photogenic French Bulldog actor/model known as Linus, who played the role of "Shakespeare," Linus is filmed sporting an Elizabethan clown collar that is often seen in old illustrations of the breed. Many porcelain Frenchie figurines show the old clown collars as well. Linus has appeared in many other films, commercials and print ads, but to my knowledge this is the only film in which he appears "dressed."

Recently, many canine apparel and accessory companies have sprouted up out of the love of French Bulldogs and have become very successful due to their adorably dressed mascots! Charming Pet Charms was the first to feature their handsome pied Frenchie,

Cowdog, as their spokesmodel. They carry a complete line of party collars, collar charms and jackets for the well-dressed Frenchie. Sococo, or "Socially Conscious Companion," is a company inspired by the owner's darling brindle French Bulldog Gilles and specializes in hand-beaded collar charms for the humanitarian cause of AIDS relief. When you purchase their charms, you can feel good about dressing up your Frenchie and supporting a good cause at the same time!

Feather boa collars became very popular among the Frenchie set, and the newer "party" collars made of tulle and rhinestones were the next step. These collars come in all colors and styles and give your dog the "clown-collar" look of yesteryear, but in a fun,

updated fashion. Handmade beaded ornamental collars have been all the rage for the past few years, as have the personalized collars that spell out your Frenchie's name in rhinestones. The old standby, the studded collar, is still quite popular for the somewhat less daring Frenchie.

If you can sew, there are many pattern books for sale that feature clothing made to fit Frenchies. Check out eBay on any given day and you will find many French Bulldog models in little shirts and sweaters featured all over the books in the auctions.

There are several items for dressing up your Frenchie that are perhaps not as fashionable or as fun as the others, but are necessary purchases for the well-being of your French Bulldog. The first item I want

Above: Ch. Fisher's Mon Reve of Starhaven can't resist the call of the open road.
Facing page, top: With a Mardi Gras-style mask and ribbons to match, Ch. Fabelhaft Flower Power, "Lily," is decked out for a celebration of her success.
Facing page, bottom: Have no fear…it's SuperFrenchie! It's the crime-fighting Ch. Enstrom's Spike of Starhaven.

to mention is an engraved tag with your address and phone number to attach to all of the beautiful and fancy collars that your Frenchie loves to wear. You can find these tags at many pet-supply stores; they engrave them on the spot. You can also order them online. Have several on hand for all of your Frenchie's different collars so that you don't forget to attach the tag when you change to a different collar. There are even stunning hand-hammered ID tags available—pricey, but worth it!

Stylish coats are a must for any Frenchie living in warm climes. When soaked in water before wearing, they can reduce the body temperature of your Frenchie to a much more comfortable level and they can be a lifesaver! Doggles, which are goggles specifically made for dogs, protect your dog's eyes from the sun's damaging rays if he rides in your convertible (seat-belted in, of course) or while on your boat.

The French Bulldog

This brings us to a most important part of your dog's fashion gear. The canine lifejacket is a must if your Frenchie spends any time on or around the water. There are many different brands, so try them on your Frenchie to see which style fits your dog the best. As we know, our beloved barrel-chested breed does not swim well, so a lifejacket can be the difference between life and death. It takes only an instant for a Frenchie to drown, so please check out the many different kinds of canine life vests and purchase one so your Frenchie can enjoy the water, worry-free, right along with you!

When looking for sweaters or coats to fit your dog, make sure to check for the broad-chest factor. French Bulldogs can be notoriously hard to fit due to their bully chests. Also check and make certain that any clothing can be put on and taken off your dog easily.

So where do Frenchies go when they're all gussied up?

Costume contests are always a big Frenchie crowd pleaser. Every year at the French Bull Dog Club of America's national specialty, the costume contest is a big hit! Entrants have ranged from bees and ladybugs to clowns, cowboys, mermaids—they have seen it all!

Other Frenchie costume contests have been popping up at Frenchie meet-ups and Frenchie fun walks all over the country, and the breed has done very well in many all-breed costume contests as well. A Frenchie took first place in the 2005 "Haute Dogs Howl'oween" costume contest in Long Beach, California; the winner appeared on *The Tonight Show with Jay Leno* dressed as a mermaid, with her owner as her adoring sailor! She was a huge hit!

In New York, attending the French Bulldog meetup groups are a must to see who can outdo whom in all of their Frenchie glamour! Feather boas, designer collars and top-of-the-line sweaters are among the many accoutrements sported by French Bulldogs in the Big Apple. With all of the fabulous doggie boutiques that have sprung up, both in the city and online, there is no end to the fashions available to Frenchies and their fashion-forward owners.

Whether it is to win a costume contest, to impress others, to protect your French Bulldog from inclement weather or simply to delight you, dressing up your Frenchie is fun! And whenever you do, be sure to take photos. You never know whether your Frenchie might be the next canine top model!

Above: Commander-in-chief Spanky is the Frenchie in charge.
Facing page: Lily shows her "flower power," adorned with roses and a feather boa.

An energetic Frenchie with titles in obedience, rally and more, Lulu is also sweet, gentle and very photogenic.

3

Le CIRQUE du Frenchie

The French Bulldog, although not known as a "circus dog," can certainly hold his own in performance events, and many of them have excelled over the years. Jackie Drucker, Clinton and Verlene House, Brenda Buckles, Andrea Morden-Moore, Deb Stevenson and many others have taken the time and have had the patience and interest to see their Frenchies achieve a high degree of excellence.

Here are some of their stories:

Deb Stevenson writes of her UCD Agathe Von Den Loewen CD, RAE, NJP, CSH, RL3, CGC, TDI, called "Lulu" for short, that "she is a monkey in a dog suit, wearing a pig costume. Comical and quite full of herself, she has a passion for stuffed toys, sticks and people of all shapes and sizes.

"On the Frenchie energy scale, Lulu is probably at the high end of the spectrum. With her impish ways, it helps to channel her energies toward good rather than evil. She enjoys rally and obedience, which she clearly views as wonderful games with treats. She is the first French Bulldog to earn the AKC's highest level rally title, Rally Advanced Excellent (RAE), and has earned her Novice Obedience title with three different organizations. At the age of two, we accidentally stumbled upon her aptitude for agility, so Lulu has added agility competition to her repertoire. She attacks agility with her own special style, mixing athleticism with a healthy dose of silliness. Yeah, she jumps pretty high for a little piggy. I have her in the 8-inch preferred class for jumpers, but I swear she clears the jumps by about a foot.

"Above all else, Lulu is a sweet little dog who adores everyone, making her ideally suited for her more serious pursuit as a therapy dog. Lulu is certified with Therapy Dogs

The French Bulldog

International, Inc. and visits a senior day care center and a senior assisted-living facility. With her outgoing personality, silly antics, sillier appearance and loving disposition, she's a natural. Like most good celebrities, Lulu knows how to make an entrance, has a commanding presence and can really work a room. She gladly soaks up all of the hugs and kisses and revels in bringing a smile or a laugh to those she visits."

Andrea Morden-Moore DVM writes of the eight Frenchies that she has lived with, loved and achieved so well with in the performance rings:

"La Petite Pierrot De McKee UD, a.k.a. 'Herk,' whelped in 1982, excelled in obedience. His titles and awards included CD, CDX, UD, CGC, High Scoring Dog in Trial in Open obedience at the 1987 FBDCA specialty in Chicago (first independent specialty) and FBDCA High-Scoring Open Dog in 1987. In 1991 Herk became the fifth French Bulldog to complete a Utility Dog (UD) title. Brenda Buckles' Magnum was the fourth Frenchie UD and, prior to that, the other Utility titles in the breed had been achieved in the 1960s. Magnum and Herk were trailblazers in obedience for the Frenchies. Yes, they can do obedience! Herk was my very first Frenchie, and my very first dog that I trained in obedience, and we went all the way! Herk was a gentle soul and is still missed to this day, 12 years after his passing.

"Regina Noir de McKee CD, CDX, CGC, a.k.a. 'Gina,' whelped in 1985, also excelled in obedience. She was the FBDCA High-Scoring Novice French Bulldog in 1985, the FBDCA High-Scoring Open French Bulldog in 1990 and High-Scoring Dog in Trial in Open obedience at the 1991 FBDCA national specialty in New Orleans. Gina was a classy and beautiful girl and she took her job of keeping the boys in line very seriously. My fondest memory of her is her growling and barking at any animal she saw on television; they didn't even have to be moving or making noise. She just recognized them as intruders to her house and made sure that we knew about them!

"Ch. Cox's O'Narly Pecoda CD, CGC, a.k.a. 'Gnarly,' was born in 1990. The disciplines in which he excelled were conformation and obedience…and being just a grand dog! Gnarly was a great dog, the perfect dog in terms of conformation, fabulous movement and a personality that won over many people to French Bulldogs. He had a lot of fans at the University of Illinois College of Veterinary Medicine and many in the oncology ward as, unfortunately, he had several run-ins with cancer. The third bout finally took him from us at the age of 10½, but he was an unofficial mascot in the ward as he came every day for radiation therapy at the clinic for a month. He howled like a banshee if kept in a cage, but the staff left him to roam the ward on his own. He was blessedly quiet and he spent his time in the easy chair, as every Frenchie should! His howl was an unearthly sound; the head clinician called it 'the Gnarly noise' and planned on using a recording of it for Halloween. I have his son to this day, detailed in the following paragraph.

"Ch. Spirit Dragon's Chiisai Tomo CD, CGC, a.k.a. 'Tomo,' was born in 1995. Tomo means 'little friend' in Japanese; and his registered name is a tribute to my decade (at that time) of martial arts and the name of our karate dojo, Spirit Dragon. Tomo is the

Above: Agility specialist Gunny flies over a jump and has a ball doing it.
Facing page: Titlist in obedience and rally obedience, Bella patiently awaits instructions for the next exercise in a rally-o trial.

son of Gnarly, a blend of Cox breeding and Carol Meyer of Starhaven. Tomo was a labor of love, as I wanted so much to have a son of Gnarly who we thought was the perfect dog. Tomo was the first (and only) dog that I handled to a championship as Gnarly was finished by his first owner. Tomo is still with us and, unlike his father, he remains a little wild man. He earned his CD, but not without the typical protest. You want me to do what? I remember during one of the legs he earned for his CD title, he did the most bizarre long down. I had taken a 'tricks' class with Tomo and he knew 'dead dog.' For his long down, he laid for three minutes with all four feet sticking out about the floor like a dead dog. He entertained many and soon earned his CD title.

"Bullmarket Shogun Spiritdragon CGC, OA, OAJ, a.k.a. 'Gunny,' born in 1997, excels in agility, his specialty. Gunny loves agility, and although he had basic obedience training, he has far more aptitude and the physique for agility and is the first dog I have trained to performance level in agility. Tomo was nearly ring-ready but hurt his back at home, so he was retired from this physically demanding sport. Gunny is far better than his handler is and in the year that I've shown him he never fails to garner admirers. He is lightning fast and takes his work seriously. We have earned the first-level titles in agility and continue to work for more 'clean runs.'

"Kobi's Arabella of Windance CGC, CD, RE, TDI, RL1, RL2, excels in rally obedience and obedience. 'Bella' was acquired from her breeder as a 'rehome.' She came to us a scant two weeks after we lost our Gnarly, and we were missing a bitch in the house. We got one in spades! Little 15-pound Bella takes her job seriously as 'play police' and pushes the boys around. She is cobby and petite and collects admirers wherever she goes. Many people are on the list of possible suspects if she ever disappears! Bella, like all of my Frenchies, has her CGC (Canine Good Citizen) title from the AKC. She has been showing in both traditional obedience and rally obedience simultaneously.

"The sport of rally obedience, or 'rally-o,' is a relatively new one, recognized by the AKC in January 2005. Another organization, the Association of Pet Dog Trainers (APDT), sponsors rally competition and offers titles. Bella has earned her first-level APDT title, RL1, and is working on the second of three levels. Bella has earned titles at all three levels of AKC rally: RN (Rally Novice), RA (Rally Advanced) and RE (Rally Excellent). She is working on her RAE (Rally Advanced Excellent) title now, which is earned by qualifying in both the Advanced and Excellent classes in a single show. It takes 10 legs to earn this highest title. Bella earned her Novice obedience title (Companion Dog, CD) last year and is working on Open-level exercises with hopes of earning her CDX (Companion Dog Excellent) this year. Bella also has earned certification as a therapy dog with Therapy Dogs International (TDI). She visits nursing homes, where she brings smiles to everyone who meets her.

The French Bulldog

"Spirit Dragon's Gilbert CGC, RN, TDI, a.k.a. 'Gilbert,' excels in rally obedience and in just being a great companion. Gilbert is a rescue dog acquired through the French Bulldog Rescue Network at the age of approximately two. He was discovered in a puppy mill in Wisconsin. His history is not known completely, but at some time he did have a family and he was kept outdoors under the porch for a winter (in Wisconsin). He was later sold to a puppy mill and lived there for some time. I adopted him and, over time, little shy Gilbert blossomed into a silly little guy. He still crouches somewhat when you reach out to pet him, so I suspect he wasn't always treated nicely. Gilbert's progress will be slow, but he is enjoying being part of a family and getting out to experience the world. He is a very sweet therapy dog, and his diminutive size (20 pounds) means he is just right for lap cuddling!

"Spirit Dragon's Nick at Night CD, RN, RL1, CGC, TDI, a.k.a. 'Nikko,' whelped in 2002, excels in obedience and rally obedience. Nikko is a rescue dog acquired at the age of two through the French Bulldog Rescue Network. Nikko was relinquished by his young owner who didn't have the time for him; he also required expensive surgery that she couldn't afford. Nikko had his knee surgery at my veterinary clinic and recuperated with me at my home. Not surprisingly, I fell in love with him and applied to adopt him. Nikko also has a congenital heart condition; though present, it does not keep him from having a normal dog's life. He will not be trained in the rigorous sport of agility, but he certainly has the physique for it and he runs like a horse! His performance will be limited to obedience, which has very limited jumping. Nikko has an aptitude for obedience that I hope will take him far. He loves to get out and do new things and he loves to please. He earned four titles in one year and is close to at least one more. He, like Bella, competes simultaneously in obedience and rally obedience and he also does therapy work. A strapping big boy, he weighs in at 31 pounds of solid muscle."

Clinton and Verlene House owned Ch. Lyndale's Editor-in-Chief (1990–1995) who, at the time of his death, was the most titled French Bulldog in the history of the breed. In addition to being a champion he had the following titles: CD, CDX, UD, CGC, therapy dog, agility I and II titles, versatility champion and ASCA CD. Verlene said, "He was a true darling, both to live with and to train. We lost him at an early age from a spontaneous back paralysis. My memory is fading, but the hole in my heart will never heal. 'Eddie's' favorite toy, in training or at play, was a racquet ball. I drilled a hole in it to attach a leather handle, and the handle served two purposes: it made certain he couldn't swallow the ball and it made it more pleasant to handle the slimy thing! He would force it to shoot out of his mouth and then revel in the chase. He had invented the perfect game to play by himself.

"He loved his treat machine. It was a prize he received from the FBDCA and it was a great prop at nursing homes and demonstrations. He also played a great piano…child's version, of course! He was eager to fetch a tissue if an audience member sneezed. With the help of his scentwork training, he amazed the school kids with his ability to 'tell colors and numbers.' His fetch commands were 'Please' and 'Thank you,' so we were able to slip in a few courtesy reminders with the demonstrations, showing that he wouldn't retrieve unless properly asked.

"Nursing-home visits presented a problem as he was too heavy for the elderly to hold on their laps and too short to be petted from the floor. I embellished the cover on his travel crate and allowed him to stand or sit on it at their sides and the problem was solved. Does it sound like we had fun? You bet your life!"

Of course, there are newcomers to the sport of Frenchie obedience and rally, too.

Warren and Debbi Houtz own U-CD Fancibul Bijou Be Mine CGC, CD, RN. Debbi writes, "Bijou is our first Frenchie and her older sister is a white Standard Poodle. We also have three cats that she tolerates and

Facing page, top: Bijou demonstrates her favorite obedience exercise—retrieving the dumbbell.
Facing page, bottom: Who says Frenchies can't fly? Todd spends his weekend on the agility course and has had success in the conformation ring.

pushes around, even though the Maine Coon is taller than she is. I started taking Bijou to obedience classes when she was about nine months old and was pleasantly surprised that she learned the attention exercises faster than any other dog I had ever trained. She was quick to learn each new exercise and we didn't have any problems until we came to the stand for exam. Each time the judge approached she would melt into a puddle, then jump in the judge's face and melt again. It took three sessions of advanced beginners before we were allowed to move on to novice.

"I eventually realized that if she was tired or bored and I couldn't jolly her into being excited, then I had just wasted an entry fee. If we entered a two-day trial, the second trial was always non-qualifying. In rally we got a leg in every trial we entered, as she loves the constant feedback. We are waiting to get our last RA leg until we finish the CDX and U-CDX because I found that going from rally, where she gets lots of talk from me, to Open [obedience], where she has to work without praise until each exercise is finished, I was getting the same second-day trial attitude…the blank stare or going around jumps, not dropping on the recall and even once letting me walk the heel pattern by myself! Very humiliating!

"I was the most surprised person when she learned to pick up the dumbbell. I really didn't think we would ever be showing in Open because I didn't think that a dog who doesn't retrieve toys would be willing to learn to fetch a wooden or plastic dumbbell. It took us two weeks longer than the other dogs, but once she got it and picked the dumbbell up off the floor, she understood it all and was retrieving it at any distance. Now she gets so excited when I bring out the dumbbell that I think it's her favorite part of the training. She is now working as a demonstration dog as I teach a beginner class with 15 students, and she is wonderful. She really is a special dog!"

Mary Phelps writes about "Todd," "His name is Autumn Run's Better on Ice OAP, OJP (named 'On Ice' as he is from a frozen insemination litter.) I am the owner, breeder and handler, and if I could ever skip an agility weekend and enter him in conformation, he would have a champion in front of his name as he has 12 points and one major."

These stories should erase any doubts about the French Bulldog's intelligence and his ability and willingness to work in obedience, rally, agility or any other activities. And once a Frenchie has gone through his paces and settled into being a mature member of the family, he seems quite suited to therapy work.

One of Squish's fans does an imitation of her favorite therapy dog. Next to her are the real Squish and Manda.

4

The
INSPIRATIONAL
Frenchie

By Bette Weinstein Kaplan and Manda S. Kaplan

Frenchies are perfect for pet-assisted therapy. Besides having the important characteristic of understanding when a person (or animal) is hurting, Frenchies are ideal physically. These bat-eared little-big dogs are not too large, but they're sturdy. They're portable; they're a good size for carrying and a comfortable weight on most laps. Frenchies shed minimally and are easy to groom before each visit, a requirement of pet-assisted therapy organizations. They love attention, have wonderful dispositions and are ever-so-sweet and loving. These characters have real senses of humor, so that people often think of them as clowns. They like to get dressed up and don't mind looking silly, and they really enjoy costume parades! A Frenchie would just as soon wear a bumblebee outfit complete with bobbling antennae as he would wear a nice warm coat or a hand-knitted sweater.

THERAPY CERTIFICATION AND REQUIREMENTS

There are many excellent pet-assisted therapy organizations, such as Delta Society Pet Partners, Dogs in Service, The Bright and Beautiful Therapy Dogs, Love on a Leash and Therapy Dogs International. Our Frenchies—Gremlynne, Squish and Tank—were certified by The Bright and Beautiful Therapy Dogs, Inc. (www.pet therapist.com). June Golden, the founder, believes that the personality of a potential therapy dog is more important than his ability to perform some rote behavior. Of course, any therapy dog must pass strict evaluation criteria.

The French Bulldog

complete the obedience portion of the therapy-dog evaluation. Although she did pass the other parts of the evaluation, when we tried to work with her in the obedience exercises she would just roll over in submissiveness.

A good therapy dog should not be frightened or distracted by loud noises or strange, bulky medical and emergency paraphernalia. Nothing fazed our girl. Her desire to get close to people, to lie in their arms like a baby and to convince each person that he or she was "the one" for her, enabled her to ignore equipment like wildly wielded canes, squeaky walkers and careening wheelchairs.

Squish, on the other hand, loved to do his obedience routine. He proudly went through the required elements of the therapy dog evaluation, although he did tense up at the dog-being-walked-past-another dog part. The evaluator warned us that since he was uncomfortable around other dogs, we would have to take him to visit where there were no other dogs to distract him. That was exactly what we did. Squish also

Our beloved late Gremlynne is a perfect example. She had been used as a breeder in a puppy mill, living in a rabbit cage 24/7 for a number of years. She knew nothing about obedience. When she came to us she had multiple health problems, and as we did our best to correct them, it became obvious that Gremlynne had one goal—to make up for all of the years she hadn't been able to love anyone. After all, she was a Frenchie! Thus, Gremmie became an extraordinary dog therapist; she soothed a great number of aching hearts after 9/11 and was nominated to the New Jersey Veterinary Hall of Fame for the months she spent at the Red Cross 9/11 Family Assistance Center. She would not have been able to do all of that good work had it not been for Bright and Beautiful's compassionate philosophy, since Gremlynne simply could not

Above, top: Therapy dogs even seem to know when other animals need some TLC. Tank and Mao (unofficial therapy cat) comfort Squish after his eye surgery.
Above, bottom: A friend of Verbal's always keeps treats in her room for his visits.

Therapy Dog Certification Analysis

Taken from information provided by
The Bright and Beautiful Therapy Dogs, Inc.

A. Initial Meeting: With the dog seated at the handler's left side, the evaluator approaches the team. This step includes the evaluator's greeting and touching the handler, repeating the dog's name, walking around the dog and handler and giving the dog a hands-on inspection and attention.

B. Cane/Awkward Stranger: In this step, the evaluator approaches with a cane, moving and speaking awkwardly. He pets the dog and also bumps him gently with the cane.

C. Socialization: For this exercise, a small group of people, medical equipment (wheelchair, cane, etc.) and ideally one or two dogs are present. The handler has the dog on a loose lead and the two walk through the group as the people mill around and talk to each other. The dog and handler make right, left and about turns, and they wander casually through the crowd three times.

D. Food Aggression: If possible, one or two dogs are present. The dog is seated next to the handler, facing the evaluator. The evaluator drops a piece of food on the floor. The handler walks past the food with the dog at his side. They turn and walk back, and the handler picks up the food.

E. Walker: The dog is seated at the handler's side. The evaluator approaches noisily with a walker, pets the dog and bumps him gently with the walker.

F. Training: The handler positions the dog to his left and faces the evaluator. A 20-foot-long line is used instead of a leash. The following exercises are evaluated: sit, down, stay (from sit or down) and come. In each instance the handler is permitted to give the command more than once and can coax the dog but may not force the dog into any position.

G. Canine-to-Canine Interaction: Two handlers and their dogs approach each other from a distance of about 15 feet, stop to speak to each other, turn and line up facing the same direction and walk forward for about 10 feet.

H. Crutches: While the dog is seated at the handler's side, the evaluator approaches with the crutches, pats the dog roughly on the head and body and bumps the dog gently with a crutch.

I. Human-to-Canine Interaction: Stability: A small group of people and if possible one or two dogs are present. No medical equipment is present for this exercise. The handler and dog wander through the group with the dog on a loose lead on either side of the handler and are exposed to the following: a metal bowl is dropped behind them; people are loudly laughing, talking and slapping each other on the back; one of the evaluators runs; two evaluators simulate an argument; an umbrella is opened and closed.

J. Working with Other Therapy Dogs: The handler and dog are positioned with the dog seated at the handler's side. An evaluator/test dog team approaches the handler and dog and position themselves the same way, facing the handler and dog from about 5 feet away. The two teams hold this position for ten seconds. The evaluator/test dog team then swings around to line up alongside the team being tested. The teams hold this position for 10 seconds.

K. Wheelchair: The handler and dog approach the wheelchair from a distance of about 5 feet. The handler leads the dog up to the wheelchair and encourages the dog to interact with the evaluator. The evaluator gently pets the dog and bumps the dog with the wheelchair.

did great work, and was inducted into the New Jersey Veterinary Hall of Fame for his post-9/11 Red Cross therapy visits.

The Tank is a wonderful therapy dog, but he is often sidelined by illness. The Bright and Beautiful bylaws state clearly that a dog must be in good health to make therapy visits, so there are some that Tank misses. However, it is said that absence makes the heart grow fonder; that works for dogs, too. When Tank does get to the facilities he visits, he's greeted with much laughter, hugging and kissing.

THE FRENCHIE THERAPIST AT WORK

Of course, there is no typical therapy Frenchie. Although they all need the training and certification essential for therapy work, the dogs can be

rescued dogs, pet dogs or champion show dogs with impressive pedigrees. What they all have in common is that fantastic Frenchie personality and a love of people.

Following are stories about the aforementioned dogs, and you'll also meet a few more Frenchie therapists.

Squish

Squish settled himself in on the couch in the bright and cheerful day room. He looked around and saw that there was someone sitting next to him—a beautifully dressed elderly woman. She sat silently, apparently not noticing the little brindle Frenchie next to her. Squish settled himself in a little more firmly, clearly getting ready for the long haul. He loved older folks. He turned his body toward the woman and began to stare: "You're mine."

Barely moving, the woman used only her left eye to glance at Squish. He stared. She waited a few minutes, then turned her head slightly and looked at him with both eyes. Squish kept staring. The woman said nothing and Squish said nothing. He just stared.

This went on for a little while. He kept looking at her, barely moving, and she would glance at him, realize he was still there and then turn away. Her expression didn't change. We had been told that she was keeping to herself a great deal since she moved to the facility and that the only time she was animated was when her family came, but they couldn't come to visit that often. The staff thought she'd be a perfect subject for our Frenchie therapist. So did he. His method usually worked, and so he stared.

Then the woman began to talk, turning her head in the little dog's direction. She spoke softly and he listened attentively; he knew that she was speaking to him. She asked him why he was there.

Above: Squish on his birthday throne at his Easter Seals surprise party.
Facing page, top: "You're such a good boy, Squish!"
Facing page, bottom: A very patriotic Squish with Manda outside of the 9/11 Red Cross Family Assistance Center, across the river from Ground Zero.

He watched her carefully, quietly, and she began to relax and feel comfortable talking with him. She spoke with Squish about her children. She told him about the dogs she had had in the past when her children were growing up. She spoke about the house she had lived in as a little girl, and the home she had had before she came to the facility. She told Squish about her late husband and the dogs that he had loved.

The day room became busy with people coming in and exchanging greetings. In places like that there are often loud voices, since a number of the residents have hearing problems. That had no effect on Squish and his lady friend. Those Frenchie ears turned toward her conversation like satellite dishes on a soccer game, catching every word. Whether he understood what she was saying didn't matter to the woman and certainly didn't matter to Squish. She apparently didn't say anything about cookies, because he was as attentive after the hour as he had been when he first affixed his soulful brown eyes on his target.

It was time to go. After a cheerful goodbye, Squish went outside to water the shrubbery on the way to the car. He slept all the way home. Mission accomplished.

The senior daycare center: Squish really loved visiting older folks, and one of his favorite places to do so was at a senior daycare center. All of the people would sit in a circle to await his arrival. Squish would work this crowd off lead, starting at one end of the circle and going up to each individual by himself. This was his idea. One by one he would greet each person very gently… reaching up to give a gentlemanly kiss to a lowered hand or face. We were always asked to explain to the clients what a therapy dog is and what a French Bulldog is. We answered questions. Then we would have to put on a show. It was easy for Squish to "dance." One of us would hold a ball up in the air and Squish would dance around while reaching for it. Primitive, but effective. After that, we would throw the ball and he would bring it back, drop it and bark his special "throw my ball, please" bark. He loved his ball and was quite agile for a Frenchie, so

The French Bulldog

Squish had a good time with his rather unique dance moves, and the seniors enjoyed the show.

House calls: Squish specialized in the home visit. He enjoyed sitting with elderly people who couldn't leave their homes very readily. He brought the Frenchie silliness and that special Squish attentiveness that made him such a hit with the older folks. Whenever a visiting nurse requested his presence, we packed up his cookies, his ball, a water bowl and a bottle of water, and off we went. The referring nurse was always at the home to make the introductions when we got there. The person we were seeing always looked forward to our paying the call; it was usually a topic of conversation for several days prior. A visit was an opportunity for the shut-in to get dressed, get her hair fixed a little more nicely and perhaps put out snacks for the humans.

One of Squish's house calls was actually shown on public television to explain what pet-assisted therapy is all about. Squish gracefully hopped up and took his place on the couch next to the smiling frail woman, and the reporter asked her what she liked best about him. She thought for a while and then answered, "Gentleness. He sits quietly and listens to me. I like that." That little Frenchie always knew when he was dealing with a fragile person; even when he was offered a cookie, he took it delicately. Of course, this was very different from the way he usually behaved at home when a cookie was proffered!

Happy birthday!: We always tried to celebrate Squish's birthday at places we visited for therapy work. We would schedule the date far in advance so that even the planning for it would provide an activity for the folks. We would bring a big bowl of fruit salad for them, and one of the staff would play "Happy Birthday" and other songs on the piano. The guest of honor got a special dog cookie while everyone sang. There was dancing for all—two-legged and four-legged. These were fun occasions!

Squish's best birthday party was at the facility for developmentally disabled adults that we visited several times a month. We mentioned to the director that Squish's birthday was coming up in a few weeks, and asked whether the participants would like to celebrate with him. She said that they definitely would and that she would handle everything—all we needed to do was appear on the prearranged day with Squish and his Frenchie housemate, Tank.

Both dogs dressed up for the occasion: Squish wore his cowboy hat and bandanna while Tank was jaunty in his Maine fisherman's hat with a colorful scarf tied around his neck. We got out of the car and approached the facility, which appeared very quiet. We wondered if we had gotten the day wrong. We went inside, and then saw "Happy Birthday" ribbon decorating the inner doorway and balloons bobbing in the background. We walked through the doorway, and 21 incredibly happy people jumped out of hiding, shouting, "Surprise! Happy Birthday, Squish!" This was actually a surprise birthday party for a French Bulldog! What a wonderful thing! And was he surprised!

The large room was decorated with balloons and birthday ribbon spiraling up pillars, hanging on chairs, everywhere. One chair was set aside in front of a pillar festooned most lavishly with balloons and ribbons. That chair was completely wrapped in red tissue paper and birthday ribbon—it was Squish's birthday throne! We put him on it and each person wanted a photo taken with the birthday boy while he sat on his throne. Then it was time to open his presents. Squish needed help with that and the celebrants were happy to assist him. He got a new water bowl shaped like a bone, which was to stay there for therapy visits. He also received a rawhide bone that Tank immediately appropriated, a couple of toys and other things, and, most meaningful to us, a birthday card signed by everyone, even the people who had difficulty writing!

When Squish died unexpectedly from mast cell disease, the director of the facility broke the sad news before our next visit. When we got there, many people came up to us and said how sorry they were that Squish had died. They said they would miss him. But one woman who was his special friend came over to us and

Facing page: Gremlynne and her most adoring fan at the senior daycare center.

said that she decided to be happy that Squish had died. She said that Squish was now in a place where he was happy all the time, so she was going to feel that way, too. Then she went over and hugged Tank.

Gremlynne

By Manda S. Kaplan

Frenchies make the best therapy dogs. Typical venues are hospitals, nursing homes, physical therapy/rehabilitation centers and assisted-living communities, but my late rescue Frenchie, Gremlynne, and I had a very different kind of opportunity in 2001…

It was shortly after September 11, 2001, and across from the smoldering ruins of the World Trade Center, the massive old ferry terminal in Liberty State Park had been transformed into the American Red Cross Family Assistance Center. This was where Gremlynne and I, a high school student, would be making many pet-assisted therapy visits over the next few months.

Gremlynne was ready, perched in her garage-sale stroller festooned with American flags. She wore a tiny red, white and blue Uncle Sam hat and a shiny blue windbreaker with red and white lettering on the back that read, "Dog America!" The model patriot.

As her handler, my job was to wheel the little rescue Frenchie around so she could work the room at lap level. As a certified therapy dog, it was Gremlynne's job to allow herself to be fussed over, lifting spirits with her truly absurd mannerisms and her rather unique face—even for a Frenchie, Gremlynne had a rather bizarre little face.

After September 11, when the country was reeling from its loss, for all the days that I could see and smell the smoke from the World Trade Center, I knew that the only way I could feel better was to become involved. The whole situation changed for me once I became a part of it. During our visits to the Family Assistance Center, Gremlynne and I worked with hundreds of survivors as well as with the family and friends of those killed in the terror that renamed the World Trade Center Ground Zero. Most of the individuals we met had just returned from escorted visits to that (then-closed) awful smoking heap of rubble, dust and human remains. They received pro bono counseling, hot meals, daily religious services, help

with child care, insurance information, death certificates—anything they needed (even official Red Cross tissues). Here there was no deluge of escalating death counts from Ground Zero; there was only one television and it never aired the news.

The EMS workers on duty there reinforced the seriousness of the situation for me. Three of them worked each shift, wheeling oxygen tanks and first-aid kits the size of suitcases. Their presence simultaneously reassured and frightened me. The amount of money being poured into this place also affected me. When I realized that large corporations and prominent individuals were spending so much money and time on this effort, I knew that my intense therapy-dog work was a legitimate response. I understood why my high school excused me from classes each time I was called out for a Red Cross visit. I was inspired and my adrenaline flowed, so I was able to work harder.

The mental-health professionals at the Family Assistance Center often asked me to work with the teenagers, since I was the only young volunteer there.

The French Bulldog

One was Robert, a 13-year-old. His eyes were glazed over as he and his father returned from Ground Zero. He only stayed with Gremlynne and me for a few minutes. He was too traumatized to notice the dog despite her desperate attempts to catch his eye.

Seeing such devastation on so many faces disturbed me and affected me deeply. It was so exhausting that I often fell asleep in the car on the way home. Sometimes after my four-hour shift, I needed Gremlynne's therapy. Before I started volunteering at the center, I had envisioned something different. I had thought that it would be like the other places we had worked, where Gremlynne and I could make everyone smile—at least for a moment. But that was a fantasy.

After seeing Robert, I wondered if I was wasting my time trying to lift spirits at the FAC; the pain I saw was too intense. But later, on the way out, I ran into Gremlynne's favorite FEMA volunteer, who promptly rolled around with her on the floor. I could see that she got a lot out of our presence. There were volunteers there from the Red Cross, the Salvation Army, the State Convention of Baptists in Ohio's Emergency Child-Care Unit, the National Organization for Victim Assistance and FEMA; many came for two weeks at a time from all over the country. I realize that by cheering the volunteers up, we gave them strength, which in turn enabled them to be more helpful to the people who needed their support. Sometimes there were visitors I could help and sometimes there weren't (and nothing I did matched my romanticized dreams of volunteerism) but I know that Gremlynne and I did make a difference—and I am grateful to have had that chance.

Above: Gremlynne and a Red Cross volunteer from California inside the 9/11 Red Cross Family Assistance Center. The center was empty because the victims and families had been taken across the Hudson River to Ground Zero, which was still closed to the public. The Red Cross personnel always wanted therapy dog and handler teams waiting at the center as the ferry passengers disembarked after those visits.
Facing page: Chris, Tank and Manda. Chris loved Tank so much that he even got his own Frenchie.

So many people thanked us for coming—the EMS workers, the clergy, the child-care people who had immediately mobilized in Ohio on the day of the attack and many more. And I remember the victims' families. I'll never forget the woman who told me that no, it was okay, she didn't need to hold the dog, as she grabbed Gremlynne and cradled her like her own baby, rocking her back and forth and sobbing, "I love you...I love you...I love you..."

The beautiful nature of the French Bulldog was so obvious in situations such as this, as Gremlynne contentedly lay on her back in the woman's arms, loving every minute of it, yet knowing somehow not to get too excited—knowing that she wasn't the only one who needed this interaction. She and Squish, the other Frenchie we had at that time, who also made visits to the Red Cross Center, were both inducted into the New Jersey Veterinary Hall of Fame for their work there.

Although Gremlynne died suddenly only a few months later, my current Frenchie, Tank, continues in her tradition by bringing therapy visits to stressed-out college students. Some of them have left their own homes, families and pets hundreds of miles away to come to college in New York City, where they are not allowed to keep pets in their dorm rooms. They need us.

Tank has proved himself quite valuable, especially during midterm and finals times. His visits are eagerly anticipated and he is greeted by literally hordes of students who are cheering and trying to take his picture on their cell phones.

In the words of one New York City college junior, "Therapy dogs are more effective than any other type of stress relief offered on campus (including backrubs, pizza and ice cream breaks, sushi breaks, movies, midnight bagel bashes and other activities). They not only help with relaxation, but they bring out the best in people, creating a warm and open atmosphere for all involved!"

Not surprisingly, Frenchies prove themselves to be lovingly adaptable; they are so devoted to people that they are excellent therapy dogs, whether in a huge room of shocked and grieving people or in a tiny lounge in a high-rise dorm surrounded by hyper teenagers.

Frenchies are gifts meant to be shared—and they love it.

The Tank

We call him Tankenstein, Tanker, Tankus, Tanky Panky. There's no escaping the fact that he's rotund; even one of his online fans remarked on seeing his photo, "That dog is so round!" He is always on a diet, eating quality diet food and diet treats, yet despite supplementation with ample quantities of cucumbers, carrots, tomatoes and strawberries, he is always up for a snack.

His Frenchie body is totally inflexible. He'll sit on the floor, staring at the sofa until someone notices and helps him up to his destination. When we do pick him up, he doesn't bend in the middle. When we carry him, his legs stick straight out in midair as though they had no bendable joints. We call him a meatloaf with legs, and those legs don't always function independently. He can barely climb steps, and there are some in the house that he refuses to attempt. When he does go up a flight of stairs, he first gathers himself and then flings his unbending body up the steps, forelegs together and hind legs together—hop, hop, hop...grunt, grunt, grunt—until he's made it to the top.

Tank loves everyone and is an excellent therapy dog, although he has to tilt his whole body just to shake hands, sometimes raising one paw so high that he topples over. This doesn't faze him at all. Inexplicably, he is able to dance around on his hind toes rather like a hippo ballerina. He sings when he

The French Bulldog

know call our home to find out how Tank is—just because they haven't seen him in the hospital in a while.

This little chunk of French pastry can cause harried New Yorkers to stop dead in their tracks, squealing and shrieking. He has inspired other people to get Frenchies of their own. And he's a star: he was discovered by renowned fashion photographer Reudi Hoffmann as he was leaving a therapy visit. In short order, Tank was climbing atop a skateboard in a photo shoot for a Verizon Wireless advertising poster. On it, Tank is the cute guy next to the boy on the board.

Tank is an amazing therapy dog, just as driven to give therapy to another animal as to a human. He barely left Squish's side after Squish had major eye surgery. With Tank's lopsided, tilting head (the legacy of a terrible middle ear infection) and his permanent wink (another legacy of another health problem), any human therapy recipient would find it hard not to feel better after sharing a laugh with this dog.

Verbal

Verbal Grebe CD is a Frenchie therapist in Kansas. Here's how his mom, Jan Grebe, explains his unusual name:

"Verbal's his name; Verbal's his game. Actually his name is Gasconade Vermeer; his brother is Gasconade Mondrian. They are three-quarters Dutch. When Verbal was born, they hadn't even gotten the amniotic sac peeled off him yet and he was already dogerwauling (the Frenchie version of caterwauling). I said, 'He sure is a verbal one!' and it stuck. Also, I'd just seen the film *The Usual Suspects* and was really taken with the Kevin Spacey character named Verbal."

Twice monthly Verbal and Jim Grebe, his dad/handler, visit a nursing home in Kansas City. Also in attendance are a Lhasa Apso mix, a Border Collie mix and a lovely Siamese cat. Verbal and Jim usually contact an impressive 20–25 residents on each visit. Not surprisingly, the brindle Frenchie has become a favorite with many residents and staff.

sleeps and caterwauls when he's upset, raising his big head high so that his wails of injustice resonate toward the heavens.

Because Tank was raised with retrievers, he always picks up a toy to greet people. We have encouraged him to carry something in his mouth when he pays his therapy calls. The developmentally disabled folks we visit know to remind him to get his toy if he becomes a little mouthy (the retriever wannabe again).

Tank has had several episodes of nearly fatal illness. His extraordinary Frenchie personality coaxed the nurses in the veterinary intensive care unit to take turns holding him on their laps for days, just cuddling him and rocking him. As one of them said, "We loved him back to life!" At the animal hospital where he is such a beloved patient, he is a true celebrity. We walk in the door and the word is passed around among the 40 or so staff: "Tank is here!" People come out to greet him in their scrub suits. We walk down the halls and strangers say hello to him (not us). Employees we barely

Above: It's hard to tell who looks happier: the woman hugging Pitou or Pitou, who's getting the hug.
Facing page: Bibbitt and Beano in their wagon on their way to a therapy visit.

Verbal is registered with the local Pets For Life program (www.kcpetsforlife.com). Their requirements are similar to those of other pet-assisted therapy organizations:

- The vet completed a medical evaluation form.
- Jim and Verbal attended a pretest class to prepare them for the Pets For Life temperament test.
- The Frenchie had to pass the temperament test, which is very similar to the AKC Canine Good Citizen test. Verbal has his Companion Dog (CD) obedience title, so he passed easily.
- Jim was not exempt: he was required to read the Pets For Life volunteer manual and take an open book test. Fortunately, he did as well on his test as Verbal did on his!

The Kansas team spends about an hour visiting the nursing home each time. Jim usually holds Verbal up so that people can pet him and look into his "lovely big eyes," or if there is a chair next to the resident they are visiting, Jim will hold the dog on his lap.

Jim explains, "At 26 pounds, Verbal is deemed too heavy to rest on most elderly laps, so I hold him. I've noticed many a teary eye when residents see this little dog and recall pets of long ago. Those who have had the bull breeds are especially receptive. Sometimes a resident who doesn't normally interact with humans opens up when Verbal is visiting. One special friend of Verbal's even keeps dog treats in her room just for him! Both Verbal and I enjoy these visits and look forward to them with keen anticipation."

Beano, Pitou and Bibbitt

Claire Senecal, who founded the Love Connection in Rhode Island, has three happily hard-working therapy Frenchies.

Beano, a champion bred by James Dalton of Faberhalft kennel, had already been Delta-certified when he came to live with Claire. Since then, he has completed the training required by the Community College of Rhode Island certificate program: a 12-week course in advanced behaviors, role-playing with different populations, acclimation to medical equipment and situations and a rigorous competency exam. A temperament test was required prior to acceptance into the program. Beano is certified by the Windwalker Humane Coalition for Professional Pet Assisted Therapy and Community Canines for Companionship and Care. The latter requires yearly temperament tests and competency exams.

The French Bulldog

Pitou completed basic obedience training and got his Canine Good Citizen title prior to his acceptance into the Community College of Rhode Island certificate program. He is also certified by the Windwalker Humane Coalition and Community Canines.

Bibbitt completed the Delta course and evaluation exam as well as the Community College of Rhode Island certificate program. She too is certified by the Windwalker Humane Coalition and Community Canines.

Claire created the Love Connection for adults with developmental disabilities to help them with everyday issues like nutrition, exercise, communication and stress. She says of her Frenchies, "Beano, Pitou and Bibbitt are the motivators, the teachers, the healers. I just drive the car that brings them to the facility. Each time we walk into the room, we hear choruses of, 'I love you, Beano,' 'Pitou, come and see me first' and 'I missed you, Bibbitt!' followed by, "Oh, hi Claire," as an afterthought. That's okay. I know that I can't compete with those great Frenchie smiles and those six big brown eyes that light up when they spot their friends."

In the seven years that Claire's dogs have been visiting the facility, she has seen many changes for the better. Claire is convinced that her three Frenchie therapists have made a huge impact on the quality of life of their friends through their unconditional love and acceptance. When working, the dogs all have different styles. Beano works the room and spends some time with everyone. He is ready with a big wet kiss for each person who bends down to pet him. Pitou and Bibbitt are content to snuggle in each client's lap as they all take turns holding a Frenchie.

Beano's cure: One day Claire visited an eighth-grade classroom that had had a number of therapy dogs come by for their program designed to familiarize the students with developmentally disabled adults who are brought to the school. Claire spoke to the students about her program while Beano and Bibbitt walked around the room, greeting each person. After the presentation, some of the teenagers sat on the floor and played with the dogs.

The assistant principal asked Claire to look at a particular boy. When she did, she saw a laughing child who was petting and talking to Beano—-who was climbing all over him. The woman explained that the youngster had been having a tough time; his parents were going through a difficult divorce. She said that this was the first time she had seen the boy smiling since the school year began.

Claire said, "I recall the many times that Beano has made people smile and laugh because of his comic ability. He certainly has brought joy in his small way. What is more incredible is that while many other therapy pets have visited that classroom, Beano is the one who brought smiles to that boy's face."

Pitou's smile: Claire's volunteers take many pictures of the participants with the pet therapists. This process not only records the participants' progress but also gives them a visual reminder to take home and look at when they need a smile. They also use the photos to construct crafts, like picture poster boards for their group homes and workshops. Claire said, "Recently a participant's sister asked me if she could have copies of all the photos of her sister with Pitou. Of course I agreed, but got teary-eyed when she added, 'My sister is 23 years old and I don't have any pictures of her smiling. I can't believe how her face lights up when she has Pitou on her lap!' What joy Pitou has brought to that family…and to mine!"

Dr. Bibbitt: Bibbitt doesn't usually hang around with the other pets, Claire says. She prefers a human lap to snuggle in. This is what makes the following incident so amazing; it testifies to Bibbitt's ability to identify the most needy being in the room in order to dispense her healing touch.

At one of their annual pet-assisted therapy Christmas parties, Claire invited a friend who had

---

Facing page: Verbal, a nursing-home resident and Jim—all with big smiles.

interned in her program to visit with her ailing four-year-old yellow Labrador Retriever. Sam had just been diagnosed with a malignant tumor; the wonderful, gentle dog was given only a few weeks to live. His guardian thought the party would lift both of their spirits.

While Bibbitt was contentedly cuddling on the lap of one of her friends, she spotted Sam and his guardian entering the room and, according to Claire, "Immediately indicated that she wanted to 'put all four on the floor.' Since Bibbitt never wanted to be put on the floor, we couldn't imagine what was going through her mind. We watched her walk over to Sam, who was lying down. She immediately sat down near the big dog—with her little bottom touching the tumor! Sam closed his eyes and had a peaceful look on his face, and Bibbitt spent the remainder of the evening giving him her brand of therapy. We looked on the scene with amazement, and we all had to agree that Bibbitt is a true healer."

THERAPY DOG PERFECTION

Personality is most important when it comes to pet-assisted therapy. Outgoing, friendly and adorable animals make the best therapists—so Frenchies are perfect for the job! You don't need expensive equipment and your dog needn't have advanced obedience training. You just need to be ready for a wonderful opportunity to bond with your dog.

It's important to note that therapy Frenchies require special consideration, primarily because of their tendency to get overheated so quickly. It is essential for a Frenchie's handler to come to each therapy session—no matter the season—prepared with a water bowl, a bottle of water and perhaps even a wet towel or cooling cloth.

These loving little-big dogs are the right size and temperament to make perfect therapy dogs—and they do. Pet-assisted therapy lifts the spirits of everyone: the people being visited, the handlers and the dogs. There is very little you can do with your French Bulldog that is as fulfilling.

PART II
À VOTRE SANTÉ!

Ch. Fabelhaft Adora-Belle ("Lisette") shines with the vitality of a healthy and fit Frenchie.

5

The French Bulldog
IN SICKNESS
& IN HEALTH

By Janice Grebe, PhD

Though arguably the cutest and sweetest-natured of canines, French Bulldogs, like other breeds, have some structural features that can predispose them to problems, and they also have a higher incidence of some diseases than other breeds do. Health surveys conducted by the French Bull Dog Club of America in 1991 and in 2000 found that the most common disorders reported in French bulldogs were, in order of incidence:

Bones and joints: Hemivertebrae/butterfly vertebrae, patellar luxation, hip dysplasia and premature intervertebral disc degeneration.

Airway and teeth: Cleft palate, elongated soft palate, stenotic nares and other airway problems, abnormal teeth.

Eye disorders: Retinal dysplasia, cherry eye, everted third eyelid, entropion, extra eyelashes. (Note: the retinal dysplasia reports were confined to a single family; this does not appear to be widespread in the breed.)

Skin disorders: Atopic dermatitis, other skin problems.

Cancer: Mast cell cancer, lymphoma, other cancers.

Reproductive system: Uterine inertia, undescended testicles.

The Frenchie owners who responded to the survey's question: "What are the three most important diseases of the French Bulldog?" listed spinal conditions, brachycephalic syndrome (airway problems), allergies and orthopedic conditions as being the most important, with behavior, epilepsy, autoimmune disorders, cardiovascular problems, reproductive problems and cancer as less common concerns.

Here are some things that you should know about your dog. You should also discuss the following things with your vet, especially if he is not experienced in caring for Frenchies, so that working together you can identify and resolve any problems as soon as they arise. Each major body system will be considered in terms of its potential for problems in Frenchies.

These cautionary notes about French Bulldog health are not meant to scarc people and dissuade them from getting a Frenchie. It is hoped that this information will inform new and potential Frenchie owners of the issues for which they should be aware and vigilant, so that if any problems do arise they will be able to spot them early on when they are most treatable. Frenchies, like orchids, are well worth the extra effort.

BONES AND JOINTS

The French Bulldog is a "dwarf" breed, which means that it has a developmental defect called chondrodystrophy. This condition affects the way that the cartilage of the fetal skeleton is replaced by bone. Chondrodystrophy gives French Bulldogs their characteristic stocky build, but in most other breeds it is considered a disease. Though there are variations of this abnormal cartilage development in some other breeds (Dachshunds, for example), in Frenchies it produces the short face, the stout limb bones that are slightly flared at the ends, the short body and the short tail that Frenchie fanciers find so desirable. Unfortunately, chondrodystrophy produces some unwanted side effects along with these aesthetically pleasing features.

Spine

The shortened body of the Frenchie is caused by the shortening of the individual vertebrae, not by a reduction in the number of vertebrae in the spine. In addition to their block-like vertebrae being considerably shorter than those of other breeds, Frenchies have a very high incidence of malformed vertebrae, most commonly manifested as wedge-shaped hemivertebrae. Hemivertebrae are usually located in the thoracic spine (the rib-bearing region) and appear to be extremely common in Frenchies. Hemivertebrae seldom cause clinical problems in dogs over the age of one year, but often a vet will notice them on an x-ray and assume that any symptomatic "back problems" are being caused by the abnormal vertebrae. However, this is not usually the case. When a Frenchie develops pain, hind limb weakness, diminished reflexes in the rear (and, if very severe, loss of sensation and incontinence of bladder and bowel), this is more likely to be the result of a herniated disc. As happens with Dachshunds, chondrodystrophy produces abnormal cartilage in the cushion-like discs between the vertebrae, causing them to degenerate early in the dog's life. In too many cases a degenerated disc will break open and allow its contents to spurt out or herniate. Though sometimes this occurs in the neck region, it most often happens around the junction between the thoracic and lumbar regions. Discs usually herniate in Frenchies at age five years (plus or minus a year) but it can occur earlier or later in some cases. Speedy diagnosis and treatment are necessary in order to avoid permanent spinal-cord damage.

If a dog suddenly shows pain (especially when the vet presses on the spine), hind limb weakness or paralysis and altered reflexes in the hind legs, the treatment should be immediate steroids and strict crate rest for several weeks. If the dog worsens despite this treatment, and especially if he becomes incontinent and loses sensation in the hind limbs, surgical removal of the herniated disc must be done if permanent spinal-cord damage is to be avoided.

Hips

Hip joints have two main components: the bony "ball and socket" and the ligaments that surround and stabilize it. In Frenchies and in other chondrodystrophic breeds it's not unusual for one of these components to be deficient in some way. If the socket is shallow, or the "ball" is flattened, these bone

Facing page: Am./Can. Ch. Daulokkes Madamoiselle J'Adore and Am./Can. Ch. Robobull Fabelhaft Xcelsior have the stocky bodies and short faces so desirable in the breed.

deficiencies can be seen on an x-ray (preferably taken after the dog is at least six months old). However, if the ligaments are loose, then a bony joint that starts out normal may permit abnormal movement that, over time, can wear the bony parts down and cause them to become abnormal (dysplastic, from the Greek meaning "bad form"). That's why a dog must be two years old or older before he can be accepted in the hip registry of the Orthopedic Foundation for Animals (OFA). As of the end of 2005, 354 Frenchies had been entered in the OFA's hip registry. Of those, 232 were normal, 7 borderline and 115 abnormal or dysplastic. Of the abnormal ones, 68 showed mild dysplasia, 37 were moderate and 10 were severe.

However, Frenchies may have dysplastic hips without showing symptoms of the degenerative arthritis that such a condition leads to in larger and heavier breeds. The massive muscles around the hip can compensate for lax ligaments and a shallow socket by holding the hip tightly together during movement. Also, Frenchies' lighter weight puts less stress on their joints. If a Frenchie should develop severely arthritic hips due to hip dysplasia, a relatively simple surgery that can relieve the pain and restore normal function is called a femoral osteotomy, in which the head of the femur (the "ball") is surgically removed. This generally gives excellent results in dogs weighing less than 50 pounds.

Hip dysplasia is a complicated condition because it's partly inherited as the result of the interaction of several different genetic factors (polygenic), partly nutritional and related to growth rate and partly related to exercise. Two parents with normal hips may produce a puppy with dysplastic ones, and one or both parents can have dysplasia and produce a pup with normal hips. However, it is generally felt that over many generations the hips in a breeder's line will gradually improve if individuals with normal hips are selectively bred.

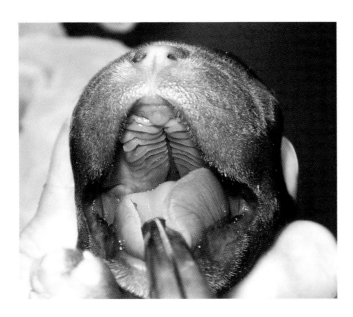

Knees (Stifles)

Like hip dysplasia, patellar luxation ("slipping kneecaps") is fairly common, particularly in smaller dogs. Though one leg may be worse than the other, both knees are usually involved to some degree. Normally the patella and the ligament in which it is embedded ride up and down in a groove on the front of the thighbone, or femur, when the leg bends or straightens. Side ligaments tether the patella at both sides of the knee, keeping it seated in the groove. However, if the groove is shallow, and/or the side ligaments are weak and slack, the patella can jump out of the groove (this is known as luxation). In Frenchies, the medial (toward the midline) ligament is most often the problem, causing the patella to displace to the inner side of the knee joint.

The severity of patellar luxation varies. In a very mild case the owner or vet can push the patella out of the groove by putting gentle thumb pressure on it while the knee is in motion, but when the knee is not being artificially manipulated, the patella stays in place. In other cases the patella may luxate on its own occasionally when the dog is gaiting, and the only evidence is that every now and then the dog will take a little skip or hop. Frenchies' massive thigh muscles can often compensate for stifle faults, as they can for hip faults, and minor luxations of this sort are not likely to have any serious consequences unless they worsen with time. However, if the knee "locks up" often or the dog shows pain, limps or carries the leg, then a surgical repair should be done. If a serious luxation goes untreated, it can cause the leg bones to become deformed and can produce an abnormal gait.

The Orthopedic Foundation for Animals has a patella registry; dogs must be 12 months of age or older in order to be entered. The inheritability of this condition is not clear, but it is generally advised to avoid breeding dogs with symptomatic luxating patellas.

RESPIRATORY PROBLEMS AND ANESTHESIA RISKS

Frenchies are a brachycephalic (brachy = "short"; cephalos = "skull") breed. The short face that makes Frenchies irresistibly cute also alters the structure of the airway and makes their breathing less efficient. Though most Frenchies do well in moderate temperatures and when not overly taxed by physical exercise or emotional stress, they all need to be kept cool since their airways lack the cooling capabilities that other breeds have. Anesthesia is also riskier in brachycephalic breeds, so extra care must be taken in administering anesthesia to a Frenchie. If the need arises, you must ensure that the person in charge of your Frenchie's anesthesia is aware of these risks and has a lot of experience with anesthetizing short-faced breeds like the Frenchie, Bulldog and Pug.

A Frenchie who is being anesthetized must have an endotracheal tube that is the proper length. The Frenchie's shorter neck sometimes means that a tube of proper length for a breed of the same size may be too long for a Frenchie and may extend into a bronchus instead of having its tip in the trachea. The diameter of the tube should be appropriate for the dog's trachea, and this may be narrower than normal. Moreover, when determining the amount of anesthesia to use, it should be taken into account that many Frenchies

Above: A cleft palate, not uncommon among the brachycephalic breeds.
Facing page: Tansey is getting an oatmeal massage for her itchy skin.

require less anesthesia than more active breeds and may eliminate anesthesia more slowly from their systems. After anesthesia, a Frenchie must lie on his belly to keep his large tongue from relaxing and clogging up his throat. You cannot be too careful with a French Bulldog undergoing anesthesia.

In addition to the need for all Frenchies to avoid extreme heat and stress, some Frenchies have one or more structural problems that are collectively called the "brachycephalic syndrome." This too-common health problem is often unrecognized and its seriousness underappreciated. In brachycephalic syndrome, the nares (nostrils) may be stenotic (pinched), the nasal cavities are often quite cramped, the soft palate may be abnormally long, the trachea may be abnormally narrow and the cartilage rings that keep the trachea open may be abnormally soft. To complicate matters, when the dog breathes strenuously, the tissues lining the airway become irritated and swollen because of the extra effort required to move air, further narrowing the airway. Any obstruction within the upper airway causes its walls to be "sucked" inward. Pinch your nose shut and try inhaling, and you can feel this happening in your own throat.

If a dog has one or more of the components of brachycephalic syndrome, prolonged airway obstruction over time pulls inward on the larynx (voicebox), and this will cause a pair of little membrane outpocketings in the larynx (the laryngeal saccules or ventricles) to turn inside-out (become everted) so that they stick into the cavity of the larynx. This is the first stage of laryngeal collapse and can suffocate the dog if these everted saccules are pulled into the opening between the vocal cords. Ongoing airway obstruction, if not corrected, can cause the walls of the box-like larynx to buckle inward, which can be fatal.

A Frenchie who is a very noisy breather, who gags and throws up foam following stress or exercise, who over-

heats easily in cool weather and takes overly long to cool down or who shows any signs of breathing trouble should be examined as soon as possible by a vet experienced with brachycephalic breeds before secondary changes in the larynx occur. This must be done under anesthesia; the owner should agree beforehand that if any problems are found, they should be surgically corrected during that same anesthesia. As anesthesia is a higher risk with these breeds, the aim is to minimize the number of times that a Frenchie is anesthetized. During surgery, nares can be enlarged, everted laryngeal saccules can be removed and an elongated soft palate can be shortened. If these procedures are done early on, you can avoid the tragedy of a fatal laryngeal collapse.

SKIN

Allergies are one of the most common and also one of the most frustrating ailments in dogs of all sorts, including Frenchies. There are three main types of canine allergies—flea allergy dermatitis, atopy and food allergy—and a dog may have more than one of them. Since fleas can now be controlled and even eliminated,

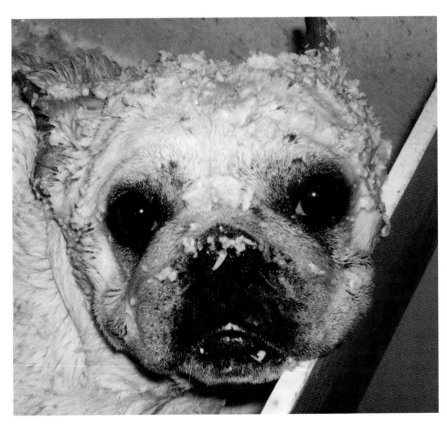

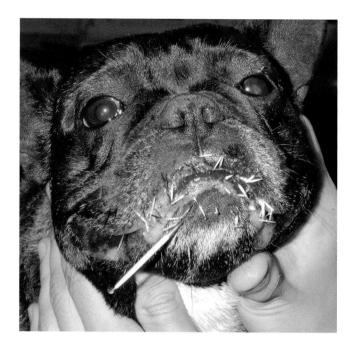

to seasonal allergens like pollen or spores, and use of an antihistamine like Benedryl or Tavist (plain Tavist, not Tavist-D) during the times when these allergens are in the air will help. A new drug containing cyclosporine is also available to control atopy, and this might be of benefit if an over-the-counter antihistamine is not sufficient. Steroids like prednisone are sometimes used to suppress the immune system's response to allergens, but long-term use of steroids is not advised because of their side effects. The use of steroids must be supervised by a veterinarian. For a dog with major allergy problems, consultation with a specialist in veterinary dermatology/immunology is advised. Sometimes an allergic dog can be tested to identify the specific substances to which he is allergic, and a series of desensitization injections given.

flea allergy dermatitis should be a thing of the past. Frenchies' biggest skin problem is atopic dermatitis. Atopy is an allergy to inhaled substances (allergens), which in humans causes sneezing, runny eyes and runny noses (symptoms known collectively as allergic rhinitis). In dogs this type of allergy usually causes skin problems (though a few dogs respond in the same way as humans, with allergic rhinitis).

A smaller number of dogs have food allergies, which can cause gastrointestinal problems, skin problems or both. An itchy dog, regardless of what allergens (inhaled or food) cause him to itch, will scratch. Scratching breaks the skin, opening the door to infection by bacteria and fungi. Infection increases the itching, and thus the scratching, and a vicious cycle is established. To break it, the owner must clear up any infection, reduce the itching so as to reduce the scratching and then determine and try to eliminate the cause of the itching.

Few conditions cause as much misery for dogs and their owners as do allergies. Some dogs are allergic only

Even in a dog without allergic skin disease, a Frenchie's exuberant supply of wrinkles and folds can form deep grooves and pockets where air circulation is reduced, creating a warm, dark, moist environment that is an open invitation to microorganisms. The resulting skin-fold dermatitis most often develops between the toes (interdigital pyoderma); in the deep grooves on the face, where tear spillover can increase the moisture problem; and in bitches in the deep folds next to the vulva. This is particularly a problem in warm, humid climates and in summertime.

Prevention is the key, so regular cleansing and drying of the folds is needed. Flushable bathroom wipes are excellent for cleaning the folds. After cleansing, the folds should be dried, and if there is any indication of broken skin or an infection, an antibiotic ointment should be applied with a cotton swab. If this does not clear it up, ask your vet to culture whatever organism(s) may be growing there and to determine their sensitivities and resistances to different antibiotic and antifungal agents. Oral antibiotics should be avoided if possible, as topical ointments should take care of the problem if properly used.

Above: This poor Frenchie came away with some painful mementos after a meeting with a porcupine.
Facing page, top: Distinct parts of that unmistakable Frenchie look, the facial folds and wrinkles need special attention to their cleanliness.
Facing page, bottom: The Frenchie is *not* a water dog!

DIGESTIVE

Vomiting, diarrhea and constipation are common problems in all breeds of dog as well as in mixed breeds, and tend to show up in dogs of all ages but usually from different causes. A gastrointestinal problem in a young puppy may well be caused by some type of birth defect. In middle-aged dogs, an infectious disease or inflammatory condition may be the cause. In senior dogs, a malignancy may be more likely.

Vomiting and Regurgitation

When a Frenchie regurgitates or vomits more than just occasionally, you need to determine what is causing it. This will require some observation on your part so that you can give your vet an accurate history of the problem.

If a Frenchie tends to throw up foam and froth, particularly after being stressed or exercised and especially if he has noisy and labored breathing in these circumstances, then the first thing to rule out is an elongated soft palate (see discussion of brachycephalic syndrome). When a dog with a compromised airway pants he salivates, and the overly long soft palate tends to whip the saliva into a froth, which the dog swallows. This froth tends to irritate the stomach and comes back up as foam.

Regurgitation, on the other hand, is the ejection of undigested food before it reaches the stomach. It tends to occur suddenly, without warning, and rather effortlessly. The dog does not feel ill, does not seem to mind and is often ready to eat again right away (and may try to re-eat the regurgitated material, which is unpleasant for most owners). What comes up appears virtually unchanged from what went down, except for having been chewed, because it never reached an area where digestion occurs.

Megaesophagus is the most common cause of regurgitation in dogs and is a secondary effect of several other conditions that interfere with the muscle activity in the lower esophagus and at its junction with the stomach. If food does not move normally down the esophagus and into the stomach, but accumulates in the esophagus, over time the esophagus becomes greatly stretched and dilated and a large amount of food can accumulate there before being regurgitated. This can be a congenital problem that begins in puppyhood, in which case it is thought to be caused by an abnormality of the nerve that controls contractions of the esophagus. It can also develop later in life as a side effect of either some neurologic problem or a problem with the muscles. Whatever the cause, it is a serious problem. A dog with megaesophagus requires special care that may include small feedings of high-calorie food of a slurry-like consistency and feeding from an elevated bowl to allow gravity to assist in swallowing and medications. Vigilance by the owner is required because frequent regurgitation can also cause aspira-

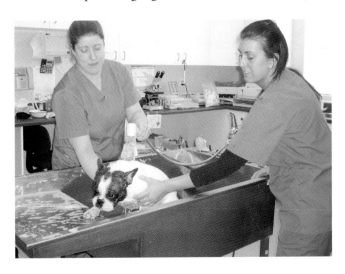

tion of material into the lungs, resulting in aspiration pneumonia.

Occasionally a Frenchie will be born with an abnormal blood vessel called a vascular ring, which encircles and constricts the lower end of the esophagus. This is caused by the persistence of a fetal blood vessel that normally disappears before birth. A vascular ring can interfere with passage of food into the stomach, causing the dog to regurgitate. If a French Bulldog puppy regurgitates frequently after weaning, a vascular ring should be considered as one possible cause.

In contrast to regurgitation, a dog who vomits generally appears to feel ill beforehand. Pacing, retching, salivating, gulping air and forceful abdominal contractions usually precede or accompany the vomiting itself. Occasional bouts of vomiting should be treated with a 24-hour fast (giving the dog liquids only to prevent dehydration), after which the dog is started back on a bland food. Repeated vomiting over a period of time or vomiting accompanied by abdominal pain can have many causes, some very serious, and should be investigated by your vet.

If a puppy experiences "projectile vomiting" soon after he begins eating solid food, the most likely cause is a congenital malformation called pyloric stenosis. The pyloric valve is a narrowing of the far end of the stomach that controls the movement of food from the stomach to the small intestine. If it is abnormally small or tight (stenotic), food accumulates in the stomach but is unable to pass through to the gut. After a time the stomach will expel the food forcefully upward. Repeated vomiting in a puppy after weaning should be checked out right away, as aspiration pneumonia is always a risk. Either an x-ray taken following a barium swallow or an endoscopic exam will diagnose this, and a simple surgical procedure is usually very successful.

Older dogs may tend to vomit small amounts of digestive juices, a clear yellowish liquid, in the morning. Oftentimes, feeding the dog a small amount at bedtime will resolve this. If not, it may be associated with a more generalized gastrointestinal disorder, inflammatory bowel disease (IBD). If a bedtime snack doesn't help, your vet may want to try some acid-reducing medication and/or a drug that alters the movements of the GI tract.

Some Frenchies tend to indulge in dietary indiscretions whenever possible, one of the more upsetting of which is coprophagia (stool eating). Few things upset owners as much as this, and volumes have been written about it. Though it seems to be more common in some lines of dog than in others, it is not clear what this means in terms of its inheritability, because there seem to be many factors involved. Many Frenchies also find long-dead things irresistible, which can result in some pretty unsettling messes. Vomiting due to these ingestions, however, is episodic and not a chronic situation.

Intestinal Problems

Room-clearing flatulence is common in Frenchies. Sometimes it's related to diet; also, a dog that pants a lot and gulps air because of a bad airway may be passing more air through his gastrointestinal tract than normal. But it's also just common in Frenchies, so if simple solutions like dietary changes don't help, just consider it a small price to pay for having a Frenchie in your life.

Constipation is not generally a problem with Frenchies, and is more common in older dogs than in young ones. Given a diet appropriate to the dog, most healthy young Frenchies defecate regularly and normally. If a dog is confined in a small space, he may voluntarily refrain from defecating, which will cause his stool to become drier and harder. If a dog's anal glands are impacted or abscessed (which some feel is more common in screw-tailed dogs if the tail's bending compresses an anal-gland duct), he may retain his stool because of pain on defecation. A neurologic condition such as might be caused by a herniated disc can cause fecal retention, as can a life-threatening mechanical obstruction of the gut by various abnormalities (tumors, adhesions, enlarged prostate, etc.).

Diarrhea may be acute, with frequent watery, sometimes bloody, stool, which may be accompanied by vomiting, pain, fever and/or loss of appetite. Chronic diarrhea is more variable; it can start gradually or suddenly or can occur intermittently. Whichever is the case, prevention of dehydration is essential. If the lining of your dog's mouth feels "tacky" instead of nice and moist, and if when you pinch up a fold of skin it remains "tented" for a bit instead of flattening when released, the dog is dehydrated and you must take immediate action.

Acute diarrhea is usually transitory. If you withhold food for 24 hours but make sure that the dog drinks plenty of water, he usually recovers. It's best to feed a bland, low-fat diet divided into several small portions daily when you begin feeding the dog again, phasing him gradually back onto his regular food. If the diarrhea continues, recurs frequently or becomes chronic, then a thorough medical workup is needed to determine the cause and devise an appropriate treatment. Before going to the vet, you should make a list of your observations as to how the diarrhea happens, when it happens, what it looks/smells like and any other information about the dog and his living situation. This will help the vet with a diagnosis.

Inflammatory bowel disease (IBD) occurs in Frenchies and must be managed medically and dietarily for the life of the dog. One type of IBD, histiocytic ulcerative colitis, is fairly common in Boxers, and has recently been reported in Frenchies (though its true incidence is not known, since an intestinal biopsy is required for accurate diagnosis). These chronic diseases require that the owner work closely with his vet and be very compliant with medical and dietary treatments.

EARS, EYES AND TEETH

The most common kind of deafness in Frenchies occurs in pied and white dogs and is a side effect of the absence of pigment in a small region within the inner ear. Deafness in only one ear will go unnoticed by the owner and can only be diagnosed with a special diagnostic test called a BAER (brainstem auditory evoked response) test. Other types of deafness do not seem related to coat color. If you have a deaf dog, you will need to adapt to his special needs, and there are many books, web sites and other sources of information that can help you.

Besides deafness, Frenchies sometimes get ear-canal infections (otitis externa). Often these ear infections are the only manifestation of atopy (allergy to inhaled substances), and they can become a major problem if not diagnosed, controlled and treated properly. If your Frenchie is scratching his ear, and especially if there is an odor or discharge, have your vet examine the ear before you attempt to clean it; this is to make sure that the eardrum is not broken. If the eardrum is fine, have the vet give you a good ear cleaner, appropriate to the type of problem that your Frenchie is experiencing, and ask him to show you how to use it properly.

Routine inspection and cleaning of the ears can prevent more serious problems from developing. Never stick cotton swabs in your Frenchie's ear at any time. You run the risk of irritating the delicate lining of the ear canal and, if any problems exist, of worsening them.

Because Frenchies tend to have rather prominent eyes, they are more vulnerable to injury. Sometimes extra eyelashes on the inside of the lid (distichiasis) or a turned-in lid margin (entropion) will cause the lashes to rub against the cornea (the clear outermost layer on the front of the eyeball). Entropion and extra lashes should be corrected to prevent chronic irritation and damage to the cornea. If the surface of the eye dries out because the dog's lids do not completely cover it (as is the case with some really bulging eyes) or because an autoimmune condition causes the tear glands to secrete insufficient tears, then the nerve fibers in the cornea can be damaged and the normally highly sensitive cornea loses its sensation. That means that any little irritation of the cornea will not cause the usual response of tearing, squinting and pawing at the irritated eye, which gives an early warning of a problem. The unnoticed corneal erosion can then progress to a larger and deeper ulcer; the first sign of this may be when a cloudiness (caused by edema) develops. This is an emergency and the dog should be treated immediately, preferably by a specialist in veterinary ophthalmology. If your own vet treats it, then you should see improvement within a few days. If a week or, at most, two weeks pass and it has not improved (or if it worsens), immediately consult an ophthalmologist, as sometimes more aggressive treatment is needed to prevent deepening of the ulcer, which can progress to rupture and loss of the eye. If there is a corneal ulcer present, do not use any ointment or drops containing a steroid (betamethasone, cortisone, etc.), as steroids can interfere with healing and worsen the problem.

Though some Frenchies have "good bites," those short little jaws simply do not accommodate the usual canine assortment of 42 teeth as well as the jaws of a long-muzzled dog do. That means that some teeth may be crowded together and even stick out at odd angles,

Above: A healthy Frenchie with clean ears, clear eyes and a correctly formed undershot jaw.
Facing page: While many health problems are possible in the breed, responsible breeders dedicate themselves to producing healthy dogs that make wonderful companions.

which can trap bits of food and cause gum disease much earlier than in dogs with normal jaws and teeth. It's a good idea to begin regular tooth-cleaning early with Frenchies so as to be able to avoid or postpone dental treatment requiring anesthesia, which as we've mentioned has higher risks for short-faced dogs.

Sometimes the puppy's "baby teeth" will be retained, causing even more crowding. Retained temporary teeth should be removed if they don't fall out on their own.

CARDIOVASCULAR SYSTEM

Several types of congenital (present at birth; not to be confused with genetic) defects of the heart and its associated blood vessels occur in Frenchies, as they do in all breeds. The true incidence of these is not known, because they are often fatal soon after birth, and unless postmortem exams are done on puppies that die, the problems remain undetected and undiagnosed.

If a puppy with a cardiac abnormality survives, the vet may hear an abnormal sound when listening to the pup's chest. Heart murmurs can be hard to detect in Frenchies because their breathing sounds may cover up abnormal heart sounds. If your vet has trouble hearing the heart sounds over the respiratory noise, he might try to interrupt the dog's breathing (briefly, please!) either by putting a finger over the nares or by holding some unpleasant-smelling item in front of the dog's nose to make him hold his breath (gauze with a bit of rubbing alcohol on it often works).

Heart "murmurs" result from vibrations produced by abnormal movement of blood within the heart or its adjacent large blood vessels. A murmur does not always indicate heart disease, and there are heart diseases that do not cause any murmur. It's not uncommon for a Frenchie pup to have a slight murmur that goes away as he matures or that remains very slight and never causes any problems. However, a more pronounced murmur or a slight one that persists into maturity (particularly if it worsens over time) should be checked out. Veterinary cardiologists may include a chest x-ray, a Doppler exam of the heart to "see" how the blood flows through it, an ultrasound exam and/or an electrocardiogram to diagnose a heart murmur. It is believed that some cardiac abnormalities are inherited, so dogs with heart problems should not be bred.

Occasionally a vet who is unfamiliar with Frenchies will look at a chest x-ray of a Frenchie and think that his heart is enlarged. But unless the dog is having symptoms that are heart-related, this could well be a normal-sized heart for the breed. A dog's body type influences the appearance of the heart on an x-ray, with a deep- and narrow-chested dog having a heart that looks narrower and more vertical. A wide, shallow-chested dog like the Frenchie tends to have a heart that appears larger (measuring 3 to 3½ intercostal spaces wide) and with a more rounded right side; the heart will often be in contact with the sternum (breastbone) and push the trachea closer to the dog's spine. In addition to breed differences, the dog's age has an influence, as the hearts of puppies and younger dogs appear proportionately larger than those of mature ones. Finally, the heart tends to appear bigger when an x-ray is taken while the dog is exhaling than when he is inhaling. Obviously, a dog that's having a problem that suggests a cardiac defect or malfunction should be given a thorough cardiac workup.

ENDOCRINE AND IMMUNE SYSTEMS

Apart from allergies, the most common immune-mediated condition in Frenchies is autoimmune thyroiditis, which can cause hypothyroidism. This is most often diagnosed because of symmetrical hair loss on the hind legs, often with a lowered energy level, and is easily treated with medication. Though other

immune-mediated diseases have been reported in Frenchies (lupus, pemphigus, diabetes, Addison's disease), these are uncommon and must be diagnosed by specialized lab tests and treated by a knowledgeable vet.

NEUROLOGIC

Spinal-cord injury in Frenchies is most often caused by a herniated disc. In older Frenchies, a gradual onset of hind leg weakness can be due to spinal arthritic changes that cause a narrowing of the spinal canal that contains the spinal cord (spinal stenosis). There is also a condition called degenerative myelopathy, in which the spinal cord progressively deteriorates, apparently because the body's immune system attacks it (similar to multiple sclerosis). Though most common in large breeds, degenerative myelopathy has been reported in Frenchies and may be underdiagnosed.

Hydrocephalus, "water on the brain," is more common in short-faced breeds because of the abnormal way in which the skull develops. A hydrocephalic puppy has an abnormal buildup of fluid in the cavities within the brain, and this causes an increasing pressure that pushes the brain against the inside of the skull. Depending on the severity, the dog may die young, or may stabilize and survive. If a puppy has a "domed" head that becomes increasingly so, has abnormal movement, does not grow well and is a slow learner (hard to housebreak), consult your vet and ask whether an ultrasound exam is indicated.

Like all other breeds, Frenchies sometimes develop seizure disorders. Many things can cause seizures, and if the known causes are all investigated and ruled out, then the dog is said to have idiopathic (of no known cause) epilepsy. The exact incidence is unknown in Frenchies, but epilepsy is one of the

Above: A healthy Frenchie will be an active and fun companion who enjoys getting his feet wet in all sorts of new adventures.

most common neurologic diseases in dogs in general. Epilepsy is extremely variable in its severity and in its response to treatment, and the best thing for an epileptic dog is to have a very well-informed and compliant owner and a good vet.

CANCER

Mast cell cancer and lymphoma are the two most common types of cancer in Frenchies. Mast cell tumors can occur in dogs of all ages, anywhere on the skin and also in the internal organs, but the most common sites are on the skin of the back of the upper thigh and on the front of the belly and chest. They appear as raised lumps, can feel either soft or solid and will often swell if manipulated. The mast cells that make up these tumors release substances into the bloodstream that can cause secondary problems elsewhere in the body, particularly in the digestive tract. Gastrointestinal ulcers are often found in dogs with mast cell cancers even though the tumor is in the skin at a distant site.

A dog may have a single tumor or several. After one has been removed, the dog is at higher-than-average risk for developing more of them, so vigilance is required. Mast cell cancers are extremely variable in terms of their aggressiveness, and each individual case has to be evaluated as to the characteristics of the tumor in order to determine the best treatment. Frenchies have a high incidence of these tumors, as do Boston Terriers, Bulldogs, Boxers and Shar-Pei. The fact that they are more common in some breeds than in others suggests a genetic component, but little is known about whether they are inheritable in any predictable way.

Lymphoma (lymphosarcoma) usually appears in older dogs and is a common malignancy in dogs of all sorts. Most often an apparently healthy dog will develop painless swellings under the skin, which are enlarged lymph nodes. Without treatment, a dog with lymphoma will only live a couple of months from the time of diagnosis. There are chemotherapy regimens available; these are changing so rapidly that consultation with a veterinary cancer specialist is recommended to see what course of action would be best.

REPRODUCTION

Cryptorchidism ("hidden testis/testes" or failure of one or both testes to descend into the scrotum) may be unilateral (monorchidism, affecting one testis) or bilateral (affecting both). A testis that fails to descend should be surgically removed, as it is at higher risk of becoming cancerous. There does appear to be a genetic component to this condition, so cryptorchid dogs should not be bred and are best neutered while young.

Pregnancy and whelping in Frenchies are not as simple as in most other breeds and should not be entered into lightly. The short body of a Frenchie presents a problem for a pregnant bitch, because as the uterus expands it crowds up against the diaphragm, pushing it up into the chest cavity and reducing the space available for the lungs to inflate. This can contribute to the inability of the uterus to contract forcefully during whelping, as labor requires energy; in order to generate that energy, the bitch has to be able to deliver a lot of oxygen to the muscles of the uterus to sustain the cellular "work" that is required for muscle contraction. Failure of the uterus to contract effectively (uterine inertia) involves several factors, and it seems to have at least some hereditary component, as there are lines of Frenchies that are able to whelp naturally. The large puppy head and narrow maternal pelvis contribute to the problem, and caesarean delivery is common for Frenchies.

Pyometra ("pus in the uterus") is actually a two-step process. First, the uterine lining thickens as a result of hormone changes during the heat cycle. Then bacteria normally found in the vagina move into the uterus and cause this thickened lining to become infected. Because of the relationship to hormones, this usually occurs within about 12 weeks of the prior heat cycle. It is more common in older bitches, which is why spaying is recommended if a bitch is not going to be bred. If a bitch becomes lethargic, loses her appetite and has increased thirst during the time period following her heat cycle, consult your vet at once, even if she does not have vaginal discharge, as this is a very serious and potentially fatal condition. A bitch who has had pyometra is most likely to have it again following subsequent seasons.

In a breed in which breeding and whelping can come with many complications, each healthy puppy is a treasure.

6

O Worthy Frenchie, BE FRUITFUL AND MULTIPLY

Not every dog is meant to be bred. Take a look at your local humane society and you will realize that there are plenty of dogs out there. Is your bitch of the quality that should be bred? Was she sold to you as a pet-quality Frenchie? If so, she was not meant to be bred. However, if you have a well-bred dog and if the breeder of your bitch suggested that you breed her, then you have several things to consider before rushing into a litter of puppies.

Is your household prepared to have a litter of puppies? This means do you have time to take care of a litter? Puppies do take a lot of time for the first eight weeks or so. Do you have the money to have a litter or do you think that you will make money by having puppies? A litter of puppies, particularly a litter of French Bulldog puppies, can be quite costly. Not only will you have the cost of the stud fee and of raising the litter but you can almost count on having the cost of a caesarian section.

Do you have the room to have a litter? They will basically take up a room in the house for two to three months. Are you ready to have a litter of four or five puppies running around the yard, digging here and there, exercising all over? If you do not sell the puppies by three months of age, will you have the room, time and money to care for them as they continue to grow, eat more food and require more veterinary services (vaccinations, etc.)? Are you having a litter to show your children "how nature works"? There are many good books and videos out there; you do not need to show them a living example with your Frenchie.

There are many major considerations to think about before deciding to have a litter. We will assume that you have thought these things through and have decided to have a litter. You have the room, the time and the money, and you have a quality bitch. Where do you go from there?

The best place to start is with the breeder that bred your bitch. Talk to her and ask what advice she has for you. She should be able to suggest a stud dog that will fit the pedigree of your female. Likely the stud dog to be used is a champion, and he may have already produced

The French Bulldog

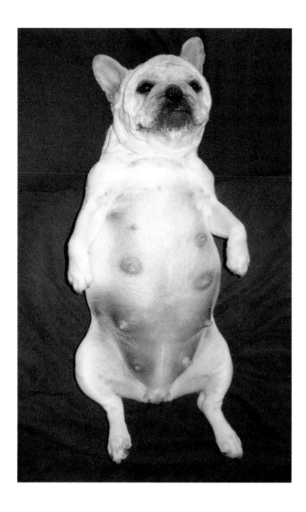

that you noticed your bitch's season. The stud-dog owner will tell you when he wants you to bring your bitch to him, as she will be bred two or three times, somewhere between the 11th and 15th days of her estrus, when she is most likely to conceive. About 63 days later, which is the gestation period for canines, your bitch will deliver her puppies. A Frenchie bitch will probably have a caesarian section, so you must work with your veterinarian to figure out when you will be bringing her in for surgery. Dogs of the brachycephalic breeds (such as French Bulldogs, Bulldogs, Pugs, Boxers and others) often require caesarian sections because of the pups' large heads and large bodies.

While waiting for the arrival of your litter, there are preparations to make. You must get a whelping box, and there are several options for this. You can make (or someone can make for you) a wooden box with a guard rail around the inside so that the mother does not lie on the puppies, you can purchase a whelping box at the pet-supply shop or you can borrow a box from a friend. Place your whelping box in a quiet, warm and draft-free room in the household, somewhere where the mother will not be easily disturbed but somewhere that is convenient for you to check on the pups often. Your bitch will wonder what the box is for and will wander in and out of it. By the time the puppies arrive, she will be quite used to this box.

In addition to your whelping box you will need terrycloth towels, a scale for weighing the puppies on a daily basis, paper towels and a note pad and pencil for writing down any and all pertinent information. The towels will be placed in the bottom of the box as a cushion for mother and puppies and will probably need to be changed on a daily basis. There are also other options for lining the bottom of the whelping box. However, it is best not to have the babies on a smooth surface where they are unable to get traction, as this will make it harder for them to get up on their legs as they start moving about.

champions and show winners. If so, you can hopefully expect a beautiful litter of promising puppies.

Once you have decided to breed and know which stud dog you are going to breed to, you only have to wait for your bitch to come into season. Do give some consideration as to whether you want a warm-weather litter or a cold-weather litter. Litters born in the spring are usually easier, as you can get them outside in the sunshine.

Your bitch will come into season for the first time between 6 and 10 months of age, but you will not want to breed her before she is 18 months old and you might want to wait until she is 2 years old. When she comes into season, contact the owner of the stud dog and tell him the date of the first day

Above: Tansey, ready to give birth to five puppies.
Facing page: Welcome to the world, little one!

The day of the big event arrives. We will assume that you have made an appointment for the caesarian and you are ready to take your girl to the clinic. Take along a sturdy cardboard box—a beer case can work quite well—and put several towels inside it. If you have a hot-water bottle, take that along too. It is important that newborns are kept warm and in a draft-free area. Many veterinarians will ask you to assist with the births, drying the pups. If asked, do assist, as you will find it a wonderful experience.

Your girl has now produced four or five puppies, the average litter size for a French Bulldog, and you are ready to bring them home. The veterinarian will help you put the babies in the box and someone will help you to get into the car with your new puppies and your rather sedated mother, who has just had major surgery. You are now on your way!

RAISING HEALTHY PUPPIES

You now have your beautiful babies in their whelping box, nestled next to mother and looking great. The first five days of their lives are the most important and there is much you can do to ensure that they are off to a good start.

If your mother has had a caesarian section, you should introduce the puppies carefully and quietly to her. First, settle her into the whelping box and do remember that she is still groggy from the surgery. Next, introduce the puppies one by one to her, showing her puppies' rears first. If she accepts the first puppy, tuck it next to her tummy and introduce the second puppy. If the mother is not sure what is happening and appears uninterested, you will probably keep the puppies in their little box for an hour or so and then try again. Show her

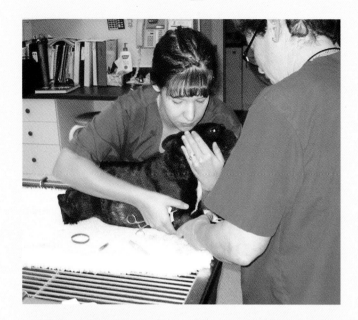 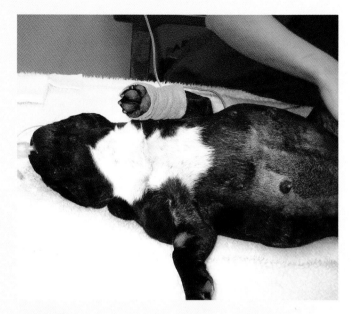

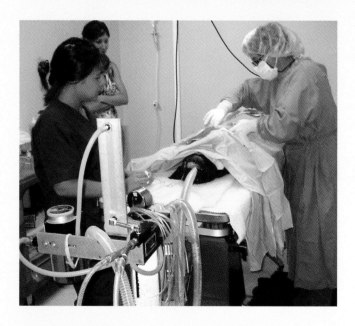 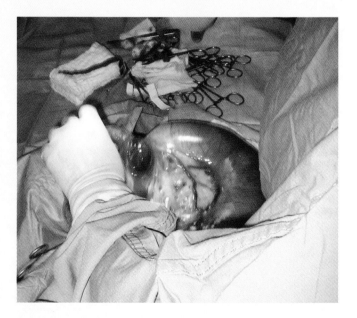

Above, top left: Setting up an intravenous line for fluid support, which all bulldog breeds should have during anesthesia.

Above, top right: The pregnant dam is fully prepped, under anesthesia and ready for surgery.

Above, bottom left: The surgeon makes her first incision while assistants monitor the anesthesia.

Above, bottom right: The uterus is out of the abdomen, the uterine body has been incised and the first puppy is ready to be removed.

Facing page, top left: The first pup is out of the uterine horn. The umbilical and blood vessels need to be clamped and then the pup will be handed to assistants for resuscitation.

Facing page, top right: Moving on to delivering the next puppy out of the uterine horn.

Facing page, center left: The second puppy is being freed from the uterus and is ready to have the umbilical vessels clamped.

Facing page, center right: Getting to know the newborn treasures.

Facing page, bottom left: The dam's anesthesia recovery is monitored. She is watched for signs of swallowing and awakening before extubation.

Facing page, bottom right: Within one hour of recovery, the proud dam surveys her new brood after a successful C-section.

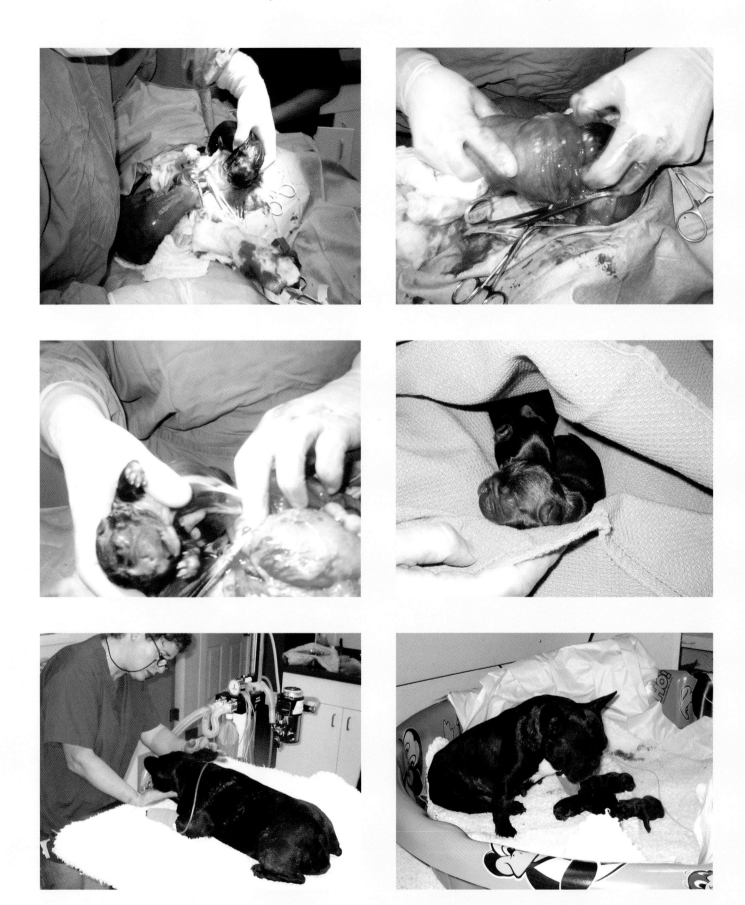

a puppy and perhaps attach the pup to a nipple and see if mom is accepting. If this is her second litter, there should be no problem.

Keep the temperature in your room at least 75°F and make certain that there are no drafts on the puppies. See that mother is drinking water and eating well and that she is taking motherhood in stride. Keep the whelping box and the area around it clean. For the first few weeks this is relatively easy to do, as mother will be doing most of the cleaning. Make sure that the puppies feel warm when you pick them up. When you look in the whelping box, you like to see the puppies tucked up next to their mother, either sleeping or nursing, and you like to see the mother looking contented and cleaning the pups as needed. You will notice that as the puppies sleep, they will look contented and their bodies will twitch.

Look over each puppy every day. Pick them up, see how they feel and check that they are warm. Look in their noses to see if they are clear and look at their rectal and genital areas to make sure that everything is clean and that there is no blood or discharge.

A drop in body temperature, no weight gain or dehydration can indicate trouble with a pup. If you pinch the skin of the puppy and it does not pop back into place, you have a dehydrated puppy. A puppy who is off in the corner of the box and feels cold (and which the mother has no interest in) is surely headed for trouble. A healthy puppy will feel like a warm glove with a hand in it. A sickly puppy will feel like the opposite—a cold, empty glove. If your mother is not interested in the puppies and appears listless or if the whole litter is crying, you have a problem and must call your veterinarian immediately. He will probably want to see your bitch and may want to see the puppies, too. Although this may sound a bit daunting, most litters are healthy litters and few problems will arise, other than the breeder's losing a bit of sleep.

If your bitch has had a caesarian section, she may be a bit slow for the first 24 to 36 hours, as she has had major surgery and anesthesia. Don't despair during this time, as soon she will be up and doing her motherly chores. During this time you should also check her incision every day and make certain that it is clean and healing properly. Again, if you feel that there are problems, call your veterinarian as soon as possible. The sutures will be removed in seven to ten days.

Most puppies will open up their eyes at around ten days of age and their ears will open up at the same time. You will start weaning your litter at around four weeks of age. If it is a large litter, six or more, you may want to start weaning a little earlier. (Actually, if necessary, you can wean your puppies as soon as they are able to stand.) Start your puppies on a gruel of kibble and a small amount of canned food and serve it in a pan that has low sides so the puppies can easily reach into the food. While they are being weaned they will also continue to nurse on their mother. However, as they grow older and their teeth are coming in, she is less inclined to let them nurse for more than a few minutes. And do remove the pan of food each time the mother is with the puppies or else she will clean the pan for you!

During this period you should trim the puppies' toenails as often as needed. As the puppies nurse, they knead the mothers' breasts, and the long toenails will be hard on her.

At the age of five or six weeeks you will take the puppies to the veterinarian for their first shots. Your clinic will tell you at what age you should bring them in and they will tell you which series of shots they will be using. You may want to take in stool samples at this time for analysis.

Facing page, top left: Mom and puppy see eye-to-eye on the important issues.
Facing page, top right: A beautiful bat-eared baby.
Facing page, bottom: Puppies are blooming! Four future Fabelhaft champions sired by Am./Can. Ch. Justamere's Golden Buddha of Fabelhaft.

O Worthy Frenchie, Be Fruitful and Multiply

Unlike other breeds, with which you start grooming at an early age, Frenchies will need little grooming other than having their toenails trimmed. A damp washcloth will clean them up if necessary. Continue to check each pup every day for any problems, but by this time you are well over the hump for a sickly puppy and there should be no concerns.

You should now be contacting the stud-dog owner for his signature on the proper AKC papers. Read the papers over carefully, sign them in the correct places and then send them to the AKC with the proper registration fee. You will now have the litter properly registered.

You should not be hesitant about placing an eight-week-old puppy with an individual who has owned a Frenchie before. Otherwise, you will probably want to keep the puppies until they are 12 weeks of age and doing well. When potential new owners visit to meet the pups, show them only the ones that you are interested in placing; do not show the pup(s) that you want to keep. Have people

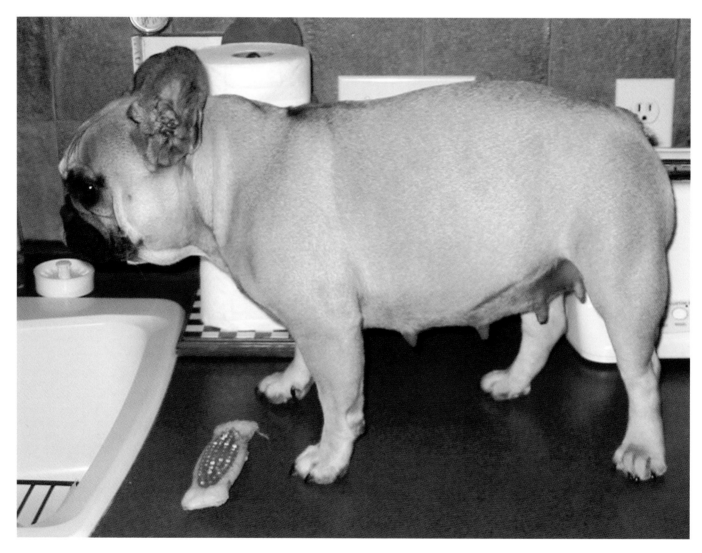

Above: A Frenchie mom before giving birth.
Facing page, top: Mom with her very young and very hungry litter.
Facing page, bottom: The whelping box is lined with soft bedding to keep the pups warm and comfortable.

meet the pups in an area that the pups are familiar with so that they look and act their best for the visitors. When a new owner comes to pick up his puppy, you will give him all of the necessary documentation (registration, pedigree, health and vaccination records, sales contract, etc.), a small bag of the food that the puppy has been eating and perhaps a small book on the Frenchie and a puppy leash and collar.

You will have mixed feelings about the puppies going to their new homes. You have tended to these little Frenchies, nourished them, cared for them and loved them, and now they are off to new homes. However, your life will now get back to normal, as well as the den or whatever room you kept the pups in, and you will once again have time for your usual activities. And before you know it, another litter may be in the works.

PART III

THE GRAND TOUR: *AMÉRIQUE!*

The Frenchie has been waving the stars and stripes for well over a century, with American fanciers being the first to embrace the bat ear.

7

The Frenchie's
NAISSANCE
1800-1930

By Anne M. Hier

It is impossible to discuss the history of the charming French Bulldog without knowing some Bulldog history as well. Although today's Bulldog is much larger than the Frenchie, small Bulldogs have always existed. These small Bulldogs, generally ranging in weight from 12 to 20 pounds, were quite popular and numerous in the lace-making center of Nottingham in England. One early illustration from 1849 shows the 20-pounder Nottingham Frank. To the casual observer, this blue and white pied dog with upright ears bears more resemblance to a French Bulldog than a Bulldog. It is from dogs such as this that the modern Frenchie descended. The first Bulldog registered with The Kennel Club (England) was also a small specimen, reportedly weighing in at only 20 pounds. So if there were so many small Bulldogs, why are today's Bulldogs so much bigger? And how did these smaller Bulldogs become "French" Bulldogs?

In 1835 Parliament outlawed the cruel sport of bullbaiting. As a result, many thought that the now-unemployed Bulldog would disappear. But since its earliest days the Bulldog was identified as uniquely English, and many fanciers continued to keep and raise the old breed. In 1859 the first dog show was held at Newcastle-on-Tyne in northeastern England. Although this show was for Pointers and Setters only, it sparked public interest in purebred dogs. The next year saw an all-breed show in England at Birmingham, and Bulldogs were among the first breeds exhibited.

Even without a written standard of perfection for the breed at the time, it was generally agreed that Bulldogs generally ranged in size from 20 to 50 pounds, and classes were always divided by weight. However, in the 1870s several Spanish imports, weighing as much as 75 pounds each, won several major awards at English shows. British fanciers reacted quickly to the threat of these too-large Bulldogs. In 1875 the world's first specialty club, the Bulldog

Club (England), was founded to create the first written standard for the breed. That standard described the ideal weight as 40 pounds for bitches and 50 pounds for dogs. As a result, over the next two decades less emphasis was put on breeding the diminutive 20-pounders.

Additionally, the effects of the Industrial Revolution on the English lace-making industry had a dramatic impact on the decrease of small Bulldogs in England. As their specialized work became mechanized, craftspeople who made lace by hand in Nottingham, where the small Bulldogs were popular, migrated to Chantilly and other French cities. And when they left, most took a little bit of England with them in the form of the diminutive Bulldogs. These little Bulldogs, many with upright ears, round foreheads and short underjaws, became the foundation stock of the French Bulldog as it developed in France over the next 20 years.

Because the Frenchie developed locally during this time and was not exhibited at shows, we know very little of any additional breeds that might have gone into the mix. Nevertheless, by the 1890s the breed had spread throughout Normandy and eventually to Paris. The Impressionist painter Toulouse-Lautrec depicted a French Bulldog at the Moulin Rouge, and photographic documentation of the breed started to appear. During this time specimens with either rose or upright ears were commonly seen; the different ear types occurred in the same litters. The breed was apparently so numerous that wealthy American tourists would often buy French Bulldogs for as little as ten dollars, literally as souvenirs of a trip abroad.

Eventually the breed caught the eye of Parisian fanciers, and several of the dogs were exhibited at a show in 1893 in Paris. These little dogs caused quite a sensation in France, but not in England. Both ear types were exhibited, and there was apparently no attempt to distinguish between the two in competition. Bulldog fanciers in the old country disparaged these dogs as "Joeys," their term for runts and weedy, poor-quality

dogs. But if France was buying, England was selling. Practically every Bulldog under 25 pounds, regardless of quality, was exported from England to France to meet the demand.

By 1893 dog shows were one of the most popular social events in England. It is extremely hard for us to imagine what excitement was caused by the introduction of each new breed to the public. Along these lines, renewed interest was expressed in perfecting the small English Bulldogs of times past. These "Toy Bulldogs" were to be a true Bulldog in miniature, weighing no more than 22 pounds. Heavy bone, flat skulls, massive underjaws and, in particular, rose ears were desired. Old catalogs show that, once again, classes for the smaller Bulldogs were offered. Because of the renewed interest in small Bulldogs, French fanciers were now shipping small Bulldogs back to England to help replenish the Toy Bulldog stock.

However, the vast majority of Bulldog breeders in England did not embrace this faddish interest in breeding small Bulldogs. They were correct in their pronouncements that this encouraged the showing of poor-quality dwarf Bulldogs that were too faulty to compete as "real" Bulldogs. Further, the small Bulldogs could be interbred with the larger animals. Bulldog fanciers were not interested in perpetuating the rounder foreheads and shorter underjaws prevalent in the smaller dogs. Additionally, many Bulldogs were starved down to the weight limit to be shown as Toy Bulldogs. To stop this cruel practice, the Bulldog fanciers established a minimum weight limit for exhibition. The dog had to be over 28 pounds to be shown as a Bulldog. Anything less, in their eyes, was not a Bulldog worthy of consideration, even though classes for the smaller weights were still offered.

This gentlemen's agreement of toleration came to an end at the Crystal Palace show in 1893 when George Krehl benched two small Bulldogs recently imported from France. Krehl was probably one of the best-known dog fanciers of his day. He was the editor of the weekly newspaper *The Stockkeeper*. This paper covered all of

Facing page: Representative of the early small Bulldogs in mid-19th-century England is 20-pound Nottingham Frank.

the shows and was lavishly illustrated with all of the top winners of the day. Additionally, he had shown champion Basset Hounds and had at one time owned the great Bloodhound Ch. Cromwell; he also had imported Borzoi from Russia. He was considered to be the leading expert on all hound breeds and frequently judged in France. With his business partner, Edward Joachim, he exhibited both the first Beagle and the first Schipperke to their championships in England. He had also exhibited champion Collies and was one of the founding members of the Irish Terrier Club (England), being instrumental in writing the first standard for the breed. He owned nothing but the best and now was interested in promoting and perfecting the Toy Bulldog.

Krehl's mistake came when, as a joke, he placed a sign over his bench describing his dogs as "French Bulldogs of British Descent." This is the first recorded use of the name "French Bulldog," and it immediately entered the language to describe those specimens with rounder foreheads, smaller jaws and larger, rounder eyes. The Bulldog exhibitors at the show were outraged that anything British, especially the "National Breed," could be described as French. Even though Krehl's dogs had rose ears, which he believed correct, the members of the Bulldog Club immediately started doing everything in their power to discourage the breeding of Toy Bulldogs.

This aversion to smaller dogs was additionally fueled when other Toy Bulldog imports arrived from France, sporting huge upright ears. Along with a button ear, no Bulldog breeder ever wants to see an upright ear. Bulldog breeders thought these dogs' appearance grotesque and were sickened when they started winning at the shows. Krehl also found the upright ear offensive and printed a wonderful cartoon in *The Stockkeeper* showing a small Bulldog flying through the air on what he termed "bat ears." Once again, Krehl had coined a term that stuck. Bat ears are completely identified as the only correct ear type for the French Bulldog.

It became apparent that if the rose-eared Toy Bulldog were to develop as a breed, it would need a separate breed club. The Toy Bulldog Club was founded in 1898 with George Krehl as a charter member. However, by this time it was too late for the breed to survive. First, the Bulldog Club had stopped

offering classes for any Bulldogs under 28 pounds. Additionally, they petitioned England's Kennel Club to stop any registration of crosses between Bulldogs and Toy Bulldogs. Without the influx of Bulldog blood, it became increasingly impossible to breed true-to-type Toy Bulldogs. Between 1898 and 1903 it was possible to register a small dog as both a Toy Bulldog and, if it had upright ears, a French Bulldog. However, the fanciers of Toy Bulldogs were trying to breed an entirely different head and ear type than that of the Frenchie. As a result, Toy Bulldogs suffered with a rapidly decreasing gene pool.

Another significant factor in the disappearance of the Toy Bulldog was a split among the ranks of the Toy Bulldog Club. George Krehl refused to allow upright ears in Toy Bulldogs. After his death in 1902, prominent members of the club, led by Lady Kathleen Pilkington, left to form the French Bulldog

The French Bulldog

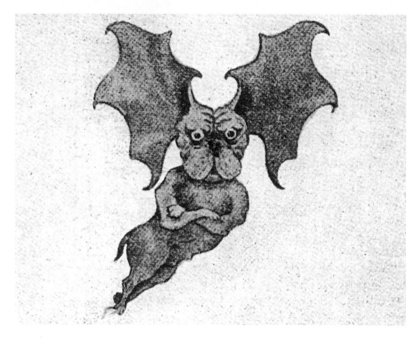

Above, left: The 1913 FBDCA national specialty, held in New York City at the Astor Hotel's rooftop Belvedere Club.
Above, right: A cigarette card featuring a bat-eared Frenchie.
Below, left: A cartoon printed in *The Stockkeeper* toward the end of the 19th century pokes fun at the bat ear.
Below, right: The winning look.
Facing page, top: A victory postcard celebrating three bully breeds with a "red, white and blue" ancestry.
Facing page, bottom: A cigarette card illustrated with a Frenchie in Paris.

French Bull

American Bull

English Bull

Same Colors and Spirit which spell
Victory

Club of England. By 1906 it had become clear that no Toy Bulldog males existed that were under the required 22 pounds. The Toy Bulldog Club petitioned to raise the weight limit to 25 pounds, and the breed name changed from Toy Bulldog to Miniature Bulldog. However, this still did not solve the problem of a small gene pool, and the last Miniature Bulldog was registered in 1915.

A significant reason for the split in the Toy Bulldog Club was the tremendous popularity of the French Bulldog in the United States. By 1896, the French Bulldog with its upright ears was the most sought-after society dog in America. The breeders in France, like the British, favored the rose ear. As a result, anything with an upright ear was sold to the American tourists. But the Americans loved the comical look of the unique bat ear and, in fact, preferred it. From 1896 to 1902 as many as 300 French Bulldogs were imported into America annually. Naturally, the price dramatically increased with demand. What could have been purchased by a tourist for $10 a few years before was subsequently sold for as much as 1,000 pounds—or almost $5,000 dollars in American dollars at that time.

In the early days of dog shows it was possible to exhibit many different breeds of dog without the benefit of registration, parent clubs or written standards of perfection. In 1896 French Bulldogs were exhibited at the Westminster Kennel Club show. There was so much interest in these novel little dogs from both the public and the press that classes were officially offered for the breed at Westminster in 1897.

Westminster hired the highly respected English judge George Raper to give the awards for Frenchies. But he judged the entry as Toy Bulldogs and gave all of the prizes to dogs with rose ears, completely ignoring the entries with bat ears. Immediately after the judging, fanciers met to form the French Bull Dog Club of America (FBDCA) and write the first official standard for the breed. In it, they stated that the only correct ear on the Frenchie was the bat ear. Confident that their preferences would now be respected, the members of the FBDCA went forward with their plans for showing at Westminster in 1898. They hired an early promoter of the breed, Mr. E. D. Faulkner, as judge and offered dozens of expensive silver trophies as

prizes. But when the club received the premium-list proofs, they discovered that Westminster had taken it upon itself to offer two divisions for the breed. One was for the dogs with bat ears and the other was for those with rose ears. Additionally, Westminster had transferred all of the FBDCA trophies to the rose-eared division. The French Bulldog club immediately protested the unauthorized changes, but Westminster refused to change the classifications. Immediately the FBDCA withdrew all of its trophies and the judge resigned the assignment. Next, with only three weeks to plan, the club decided to hold an independent specialty for the breed in the Sun Parlors at the Waldorf-Astoria hotel.

The first independent specialty show of the French Bull Dog Club of America created a sensation in New York City. First, no dog show had ever been held in a hotel. Engraved invitations were sent out for the formal dinner and dance that were to follow the show, and all of society clamored to receive one. All three of the major New York City newspapers sent reporters and illustrators to cover the event. It is said that no single event since the Civil War received as many pages of coverage. Besides super-detailed descriptions of the clothing worn by attendees, the standard of the breed was printed in the paper to help acquaint the observer with the fine points of the 26 entrants. Particular attention was given to the correct ear. This show attracted so much positive attention to the breed that within five years Americans possessed the best French Bulldogs in the world and fanciers were soon exporting top show dogs to England.

The American fanciers not only wrote the first standard of perfection for the French Bulldog but also successfully utilized the press to establish correct type in the public's eye. And for the public, correct type meant a bat ear. The market for rose-eared dogs literally evaporated overnight, and this put French and British fanciers of Toy Bulldogs and French Bulldogs in a difficult position. America was the largest market for the French Bulldog, and Americans no longer would buy French Bulldogs with rose ears. In 1898 the French created a written standard allowing both types of ear. However, classes for dogs with bat ears were not offered at their shows. By the foundation of the French Bulldog Club of England in 1902 it had become accepted that the bat ear was, indeed, one of the principal distinguishing characteristics of the breed. And it was also clear that the French Bulldog was not a Toy Bulldog anymore but a separate and unique breed of dog.

The French Bulldog's existence probably has more to do with human pettiness than any other factor. It is quite clear that the breeding of miniaturized Bulldogs was a late 19th-century fad. Had the Bulldog Club not done everything in its power to stop any breeding of small Bulldogs, it is quite possible the French Bulldog would have disappeared by World War I just as the Toy Bulldog did. But because the unique bat ear caught on with the public, the Frenchie was able to achieve separate breed status.

When first introduced to America, French Bulldogs quickly became the darlings of society. Although the French Bulldog was considered a fashionable breed in America in the late 1890s and up until World War I, very few were ever actually registered with the American Kennel Club (AKC). At the time, it was possible to show dogs without the benefit of having them registered. For example, in 1900 the AKC registered only 35 French Bulldogs. In 1910 that number was 48 registrations. After World War I, the AKC changed its rules, and only registered dogs could be exhibited. Thus in 1920 the AKC registered 543 French Bulldogs, a number clearly more consistent with the actual annual number of dogs born in and imported into the USA. However, after the stock market crash in 1929, owning and exhibiting purebred dogs became a luxury few could afford. As a result, French Bulldog registrations dropped to 275 in 1930 and continued on a precipitous decline for the next 50 years.

Another factor contributing to the rapid decline of the French Bulldog was the competing popularity of the Boston Terrier. The Frenchie was a society dog, appealing to those who could afford exorbitant prices for top prospects. By contrast, the Boston was an American-made working man's dog, available at a reasonable price. Additionally, after World War I, Americans no longer identified with old-fashioned Victorian tastes and styles. What was wanted was some-

thing modern, and the Boston Terrier fit the bill. The Boston's striking, stylish and flashy brindle and white pattern was established as preferred in 1896. His distinctive markings were perfectly in keeping with the new Art Deco style—and in decided contrast to the dour, stately, solid brindle color of most French Bulldogs of the time.

The competitive impact of the Boston Terrier on the French Bulldog can be verified in the registration data. In 1903, after only ten years of recognition, over 300 Bostons were entered at the Boston Terrier Club of America's national specialty, making it the largest single-breed specialty in the world. In 1910, Bostons registered 5,235 individual dogs, the first breed in the United States to top 5,000 in one year. In 1920, Boston Terriers again set a record as the first breed with more than 10,000 individual AKC registrations. This number almost eclipsed all other breed registrations combined, with no registrations coming from imported dogs. During the following decades it seemed as if everyone in America owned a Boston Terrier. And with drastically declining registrations, the Frenchie was destined to disappear forever as a passing Victorian fad.

Fortunately for the survival of the breed, the French Bulldog enjoyed continued popularity in Great Britain. For many years, Great Britain remained the principal source for importing quality French Bulldog show and breeding stock into the US. This stock provided foundation dogs for many kennels in continental Europe as well. In contrast, very few Boston Terriers were exported from America, because most were customarily cropped. After 1905, all ear cropping was banned in Great Britain and no dogs born after then could be exhibited at shows. As a result, there was little interest in Boston Terriers overseas. Without the pressure of competition from a similar breed, the French Bulldog in Great Britain flourished. Additionally, a handful of loyal and dedicated members of the French Bull Dog Club of America continued to exhibit during these lean years and keep this wonderful breed before the public's eye. And when the breed started its climb back into public favor during the 1970s, the French Bulldogs from Great Britain and continental Europe served as the source stock to help reestablish quality in the US.

Establishing a firm foothold in the US by the end of the 20th century, the French Bulldog is now looking ahead to a bright future.

8

The Frenchie's
BELLE EPOCH
1930–2000

THE QUIET YEARS—1930–1940

We've seen how the breed reached the height of its popularity in the United States during the first two decades of the 20th century. The early specialties held at the Astor Hotel had spectacular entries, and the French Bulldog was found to be a status dog, a breed that was bred for and owned by the eastern society.

By the 1920s the breed had taken a sharp decline; there were several probable reasons for the drop in registrations. The Frenchie was not an "easy keeper." The breed did not fare well in the heat; if not taken care of properly during the summer months, or the coldest of winter months, dire consequences could follow. Additionally, there were problems with the birthing of puppies. As with all other brachycephalic breeds, a caesarian section is recommended rather than a natural whelping. It was not until the 1950s that veterinary techniques had improved enough so that the bitch in whelp could survive a c-section. Too often in the first half of the century, operating techniques were crude, conditions and instruments not sterilized and antibiotics unavailable. In addition, litters were often small, with only three or four pups. Consequently there was not a ready supply of puppies for the public to purchase.

The aforementioned stock market collapse in 1929 and the Depression immediately following took a heavy toll on the interest in purebred dogs in general. By 1933 the FBDCA no longer held a national specialty by itself, as the entries were becoming so small that an independent specialty was no longer financially feasible. Specialties were then held within all-breed shows. Surely the Great Depression greatly curtailed breeding programs, as only the very wealthy could afford to breed and show their dogs.

In America one of the few prominent fanciers was John Maginnis of Chicago. His Lincolnwood kennels, located in Burlington, Wisconsin, housed primarily Irish Terriers and Smooth Fox Terriers, but one little Frenchie also was kept. Through his efforts in showing this

The French Bulldog

LaFrance Model II. On another note: it was noted in the April 1938 issue of *Dog News* that the solid white French Bulldog Ch. LaFrance Piccolo, owned by Mrs. Juliette Slote of Mt. Vernon, New York, died during the Westminster dog show. Cause of death was not given.

Another French Bulldog kennel, written up in the March 1939 *AKC Gazette* by Arthur Frederick Jones as part of his series of articles on the great kennels of the times, was the Seafren kennels of Mr. and Mrs. Saunders L. Meade from Sunnyridge Farms in Berwyn, Pennsylvania. Already the owners of a working farm, which had its own "dairy, hoggery, stable and poultry pens," the couple decided to add dog breeding to the mix. Sealyham Terriers and French Bulldogs, being favorites of the couple, were chosen as the breeds to champion.

Mr. Jones wrote, "As a pet it is still, and rightly, one of the nation's most popular dogs. But many who own Frenchies never bother to register them, and are content to remain away from shows. Perhaps there is a curious reason for the apathetic attitude of French Bulldog owners? To me it always has seemed that many of those who owned this breed were so interested in their particular specimens that they had no thought for the breed in general. Their attitude was not consciously selfish; it was just that their dogs had so much personality that there seemed no reason to stray from home to seek show ring honors…Possibly that is just a theory, but then I have known the breed, and liked it, since I was a boy, having a cousin who always has owned at least one Frenchie. But, curiously, in more than a decade and a half of writing articles about the leading kennels in America, I never before have written one about this breed."

There follows an extensive overview of the kennels and grounds for the dogs. The first Frenchie the Meades purchased, Beaute d'Amourette, completed her championship in 1935 at the Amourette kennel. At Seafren she produced a number of "good puppies," in addition

bitch, Ch. Miss Modesty, Maginnis helped to keep the breed in the public eye. Miss Modesty was a prolific winner, taking first place in the Non-Sporting Group 69 times and being awarded four all-breed Bests in Show. In 1936 she won the AKC award for Best Non-Sporting dog. In 1937 she won the national specialty before becoming a champion, and she won the specialty again in 1938. In 1937 she was Best of Breed over 78 Frenchies at the Morris and Essex show and repeated the win, over 90 Frenchies, at the 1938 show. She was American-bred, coming from the LaFrance kennels of Mr. Fred Poffet, and was always handled by Jimmy Sullivan. She was whelped in 1935 and sired by Ch.

Above, top: Ch. LaFrance Piccolo.
Above, bottom: Ch. Miss Modesty and family.
Facing page, top: Stud card from Fred Poffet's LaFrance kennel.
Facing page, bottom: *Dog World* cover featuring Mr. and Mrs. Harold Horton at home.

to winning a Best of Breed ribbon three times. Seafren's first homebred champion was Ch. Spiecker's Suzette, earning her championship in 1937. Ch. LaFrance Fleurette was their winning dog in 1938. Ch. Seafren Monahan Boy was Winner's Dog at Morris and Essex in 1939, had numerous Group placements and was Best of Breed at Westminster in 1940. Mr. Jones noted, "All the Seafren specimens are in top condition, and when they go before the judges this fact is distinctly in their favor. Mr. and Mrs. Meade have always emphasized soundness in the breeding of blooded stock—even before they turned their attention to dogs. But they give great credit for the present excellent shape of the Seafren specimens to James McNaull, the kennel manager. He is very conscientious and maintains a strict routine in the kennels. Mrs. McNaull takes great pride in raising puppies." Unfortunately, there seems to be no further word of this kennel, which was off to an impressive start. Perhaps the start of World War II was their demise, as it was with many other kennels. The Meades had been active in the FBDCA, with Mr. Meade serving as treasurer and Mrs. Meade as secretary.

The French Bulldog of Mr. and Mrs. Harold Horton must be mentioned, as he was probably one of the more well-traveled Frenchies. The following appeared in *The Chicago American* newspaper, dated July 24, 1939, in an article titled "Claudie Fails to Get His Femme": "Petit Claude, the Harold Hortons' French Bulldog, is home from his second trip abroad, a three months' tour of the French provinces. In all the hotels where the Hortons stayed he had room service with a waiter in tails coming up to cut up his roast beef

and address him solemnly as 'Monsieur.' Coming home on the Normandie he dines in the Hortons' cabin with the head butcher cutting up his meat.

"One purpose of his visit to France was to find a companion, but no satisfactory ones were available and so, after landing in New York, the Hortons went to Larchmont and selected a puppy six weeks old, half-sister of the prize-winning Miss Modesty…Claudie has as many pictures of himself against foreign backgrounds as any returned tourist, for Mr. Horton covered their trip with his third-dimension camera. Some of the places they were seeing for the first time, others were old favorites. At the Martinez Hotel in Cannes they had the same room for the fourth time…"

A final note on the 1930s: in the 1938 AKC Blue Book where Miss Modesty was featured in the Lincolnwood kennels, a second Frenchie in another advertisement was Ch. Ninon's Dauphin Francois, sired by Phoebe's Menjou and out of Ninon, owned by Mrs. Ramos from San Francisco. This was the first sign that the breed was moving West.

THE WAR YEARS—1940–1950
AKC registrations for the French Bulldog in 1940 were at 100 for the year. The Frenchie had now become a rare breed. The health and breeding problems were hard

enough on the breed, but with the onset of World War II there were many problems for anyone breeding pure-bred dogs. In Europe, as the war raged, breeders were no longer able to find enough food to feed their dogs. Many dogs died of starvation or were put down because of the lack of food. In the book *The Kennelgarth Scottish Terrier,* written by Betty Penn-Bull from the UK, she noted, "Some breeders were obliged to close their kennels, while others could keep only a very few dogs. Breeding was reduced to a minimum and a number of good dogs left the country. But there were some advantages, one being that a great deal of poor-quality stock was culled and those dogs which were retained were the best ones. Therefore, the general level of stock produced tended to improve, and for several years only carefully planned matings were embarked upon, and few inferior litters were produced."

Mr. Poffet and his LaFrance kennels continued to breed excellent dogs for many decades. Another of his winners, owned by Mr. and Mrs. Harold Horton, was featured on the cover of the October 1941 issue of *Dog World* magazine. Ch. Cosette de LaFrance was sired by Ch. LaFrance Model III, a well-known show dog and sire of many winners. The article in *Dog World* said, "The Hortons got interested in Frenchies about ten years ago when Mr. H. decided to give Mrs. Horton a dog for a birthday present and happened to have a friend who had a French Bulldog bitch with five puppies…later, the Hortons visited the LaFrance kennels and purchased Cosette. Cosette was shown at the Morris and Essex show, while still a puppy, under the highly regarded judge Alva Rosenberg, where she went Winner's Bitch with 43 bitches in competition. She was made a champion in short time and bred to LaFrance Romeo. The Hortons are therefore looking forward to Cosette's blessed event in October with mingled apprehension and hope—apprehension for fear that something will happen to their beloved Cosette and hope that all the puppies will be champions."

A note at the end of this article, which had nothing to do with Cosette, mentioned that a cup, 22 inches high and offered by the FBDCA, was won by Mrs. Fannie Vets of Osage kennels for Ch. Nap Phoebus, who won the most Bests of Breed during 1940.

By the mid-1940s many Americans were moving to the West Coast, and the French Bulldog breeders moved right along with them. Of particular note on the West Coast were Enid Ramos, Lucretia Bedal and Betty (Garman) Nordfelt, whose kennel names were in the background of some of the great French Bulldogs.

In the late 1940s the kennel of Mr. and Mrs. George Jeffrey of Short Hills, New Jersey was well known in the show ring with their male, Ch. Le Petit Marquis de LaFrance II. Bred by Fred Poffet, this dog was Best of Breed four times at the Morris and Essex show and winner of the FBDCA specialty in 1949, 1950 and 1951. He was Best of Breed 30 times in 39 shows and never took a red ribbon except in the Group.

Other active Frenchie fanciers during these years were Fred and Doris Carter, owners of Ch. Carter's Galopan, who won 87 Bests of Breed, including Best of Breed at Westminster Kennel Club in 1950.

Above: Ch. Terrette's Tourbillon D'Gamin CD, "Jock," one of the breed's top producers.
Facing page: The Terretts' other top producer, Ch. Terrette's Tourbillon Orage.

THE LEAN YEARS—1950–1960

The walk through the history of the breed starts to pick up during the 1950s due to breeders on the West Coast, a breeder in Michigan and several East Coast breeders. Even though yearly registrations were still low (fewer than 100 per year during the 1950s and 1960s) and the Frenchie was still considered a rare breed, the French Bulldog was being kept in front of the public eye by these dedicated individuals.

The majority of Frenchies registered and shown were bred on the West Coast. Active breeders were Dick and Angel Terrett (sometimes spelled Terrette), Janis Hampton, Betty Nordfelt of Laurelwood kennels and Ed Bigham and Bud Niles of Balihai kennels. In addition, Lucretia Bedal and Enid Ramos continued to breed cooperatively and provided much of the foundation stock for the newcomers.

The Terretts bred their first litter in 1949. Patti Adams wrote in a *French Bullytin* article, "Angel loves children and all living things. She has a magic touch with any living thing that simply can't be denied. Dick Terrett was the handler and trainer of the Frenchies. The two worked together on planning the breedings and never bred two dogs with similar faults." They knew the pedigrees and the dogs, and they knew how to put them together. There are two Terrett dogs on the top-producer list, Ch. Terrette's Tourbillon D'Gamin CD and Ch. Terrette's Tourbillon Orage. The two produced a combined total of 55 champions; in the middle of the 20th century this was a major accomplishment. Dick showed the dogs but sometimes Angel also was seen in the ring. Another major accomplishment of this kennel was the number of obedience degrees that Dick put on French Bulldogs. He estimated that he had 12 Frenchies with CD titles and another 5 with advanced obedience degrees.

Lucretia Bedal in San Francisco provided the foundation stock for the Terretts with a bitch by the name of Terrette's Mitzi. In her first litter she whelped Terrette's Chef D'Oeuvre, who was shown to his championship by the age of one year and became the sire of top producer Gamin. The Terretts remained active in Frenchies until Dick's death in 1981. Their legacy to the French Bulldog was great and their dogs can still be found in the background of many pedigrees.

Janis Hampton entered the French Bulldog world at the age of six when she was given her first Frenchie. She stayed interested in the breed, but it wasn't until she rescued one of Mrs. Bedal's Frenchies, Ch. Bedal's Caprice Nocturne, that her interest grew beyond just having a Frenchie in the household. Caprice was bred to Ch. Terrette's Tourbillon D'Gamin and produced a litter of three, including Ch. Hampton's Petite Cherie, who were all to become champions. In an interview, Mrs. Hampton said that Lucretia Bedal's dogs were responsible for getting her started on the right track, along with the devotion and help of Angel and Dick Terrett. Ch. Hampton's Menjou Le Trois was a very showy dog who opened up the door on the West Coast to Group placements. Ch. Hampton's Chevalier, owned by Foster Hanson, was another top producer who was sired by Gamin.

Janis judged many breeds and was an international judge of Frenchies, judging 248 entries at the French Bulldog Club of England's 75th anniversary show. She was devoted to the breed and worked ceaselessly to educate others. She lived a long life, active in Frenchies to the end, and was highly respected and dearly loved.

Breeding Frenchies as early as the 1940s, Betty Nordfelt of Laurelwood kennels in California owned a "huge dairy goat farm, famous for prize goats and livestock research." In her breeding Betty stressed soundness and correct movement. She preferred strong linebreeding, but never inbreeding. Ch. Laurelwood Jeep was the sire of 19 champions, and many champions carried the Laurelwood prefix. In 1956 *Dog World* magazine awarded Mrs. Betty Garman Nordfelt its Award for Outstanding Service to Dogs, selected by a unanimous vote of the members of the Pacific Coast French Bulldog Club.

Moving to the East Coast, Dick and Helen Hover were active in the breed for four decades, with Helen serving as secretary of the FBDCA for 27 years and Dick serving as the American Kennel Club delegate for many years. In 1975 their Ch. Hover's Snow White won the FBDCA national specialty and in 1979 Ch. Hover's Annabella d'Or won the specialty. In addition to the Hovers, Charlotte Prizer was also a great supporter of the breed on the East Coast.

Our trip through the decades now takes us to Ralph and Amanda West (Ralanda kennels) from Livonia, Michigan. They began with the Frenchie in the late 1940s and continued through the 1950s and 1960s. Mrs. West had the winningest Frenchies in the ring for several decades and she did much to advance the cream-colored Frenchie. Her foundation dog was Ch. Bouquet Nouvelle Ami ("Jo-Jo"), whom she purchased as a puppy in 1951 from breeder Bernard Strauss. Another big winner from the Ralanda kennels was Ch. Ber-Neil's Jeepers Jackie, whelped in 1957, who won the national specialty four years in a row as well as four all-breed Bests in Show. Except for her later years, when her health was failing, Mrs. West handled all of her dogs. The biggest winner from this kennel was Ch. Ralanda Ami Francine.

Mrs. West said, "Traveling with the boisterous champions is no chore at all. When we go by car, we stop along the way to shop for their food because they like it fresh. They are fussy eaters. Their favorite meat is pot roast, although they like steak and veal. If we go by train, we take a compartment and can keep the dogs right with us without crating. They enjoy their trip…back at the ranch house in Livonia, the dogs have their own kennels in the basement, and an enclosed runway on the spacious grounds. The house's interior is 'French Bulldog' with every room carrying out the theme with pictures and paintings, trophies, silver doghead plaques on the doors and every dog magazine there is…Traveling around to the shows eats up Mr. West's vacation with a few days here and a few there, but the excitement of the shows and the steady flow of ribbons and valuable awards more than compensates for an annual vacation jaunt." Mrs. West admits wistfully, though, "I do wish that some year we could make a trip to California—I want to see the Frenchies out there."

Mrs. West's love of the Frenchie went back to 1928, when she received her first pet Frenchie. By the late 1960s her dogs had won over 110 Bests in Show. The kennel name Ralanda came about as a combination of the first names of the Wests: Ralph and Amanda. Both were equally dedicated to the breed and to the sport of dogs. Mrs. West was chief ring steward for the Detroit Kennel Club, and both were founders of the Progressive Dog Club of Wayne County. Mrs. West was a tireless supporter of the breed even when her Frenchie was the only one of the breed to be entered at a dog show.

We have concentrated on the history of the Frenchie up to 1960, and those mentioned are the individuals who deeply supported the breed and kept it alive during the quiet and lean years when the French Bulldog was considered to be a rare breed. These were individuals with a great love and understanding of the French Bulldog. They were willing to spend both the time and the money to keep the breed alive and before the public eye.

1960–1970

The December 1961 *AKC Gazette* contained a very short article titled, "Why is the Frenchie So Scarce?" The article stated, "There are many advantages to owning a dog of this breed but there are very few bred and very few exhibited. If the trend keeps on, eventually the breed will become extinct…There certainly are some dogs of the breed that should be brought into the show ring and obedience ring where people will be able to see them and observe the temperament that goes with

Facing page, top: Janis Hampton and Ed Bigham with Ch. Balihai's Quad.

them. No one wants to see the breed overpopularized but certainly the breed deserves to be known and appreciated by the public."

The Frenchie world was beginning to look a bit brighter in the 1960s, but registrations were still very low, with 106 registered in 1960. Surprisingly, in 1970 the number of registrations had not significantly changed. However, the judges and the public were becoming more aware of this little dog with the big bat ears and the fanciers from the East to the West were, as always, dedicated to the breed and in keeping it alive.

Ch. Schmidt's Madame Patachou, whelped in 1965 out of Ch. Hampton's Jolie Coquette, bred by Jane Schmidt and owned by Betty Austin, was a top producer with ten champions to her credit. Mrs. Austin was active for a decade or so, with quite a few Frenchies carrying the Austin prefix.

Mrs. Lavender Lovell from Connecticut was a very familiar sight at the dog shows, arriving in a lavender Cadillac. Janis Hampton noted in a *French Bullytin* interview, "I will never forget the 'tailgate' picnic behind her elegant lavender Cadillac with buckets of fried chicken and all the goodies imaginable spread out on the tailgate. I can still see Laddie holding court, feeding her dogs bites of chicken and handing out chicken legs to all of us, under a wide-brimmed lavender hat that shaded her broad, sparkling smile!" Mrs. Lovell's Ch. Chaseholme Mr. Chips, an English import, was shown on the East Coast and in Canada and sired some very nice puppies in addition to doing some nice winning. Mr. Chips was featured on the cover of the October 1970 *Dog World* magazine, and it was noted that "he is always a pleasure and a joy to his owner."

A long-lasting California kennel that became well known in the 1960s was the Balihai kennel of Ed Bigham and Bud Niles. Ed said that in 1951 he felt the only thing missing in his life was a four-legged friend, so off he went to the animal shelter, where he was shown some puppies. In the back sat a little Bulldog-looking puppy and it was love at first sight. For six dollars he brought her home and they had 13 years of happiness. Several months after bringing her home, some "doggy" friends stopped by and told him that he had a French Bulldog. Ed then started attending dog shows to find out more about this breed. Balihai kennels had many

champions over the years, but perhaps the best known was Ch. Balihai's Quad, who sired 13 champions, including Ch. Adams King of the Road, a top producer with 25 champion get. Both Ed and Bud remained active in Frenchies and the FBDCA for many years.

1970–1980

The breed was still struggling and few sightings of Frenchies were seen in the show ring. For many years the average entry at a national specialty was 35 and by 1970 through the mid-1980s the entry dropped as low as 22 at a national specialty. However, during the mid-1970s registration reached as high as 200 per year, and it looked like the breed would not disappear from the scene.

California breeders from the 1970s not to be missed are Abe and Suzi Segal of the Taurustrail prefix. Originally Bulldog breeders, the Segals came to Frenchies in a rather unique way. Suzi wrote an article titled "How We Accidentally Ended Up with Duke in Our Lives!" The article stated, "One day Abe was in the yard and a woman drove up and asked if we had lost a Bulldog, as she had found one. We weren't missing any dogs but I got in her car and when we got to her house I found quite a nice brindle French Bulldog bitch. I took her home to try and find the owner. I contacted several Frenchie people and several days later someone came up with a family who lived a couple of miles away and who had lost their dog. I called and apparently the dog had been missing for some time, as the wife couldn't remember the Frenchie's name! The husband, wife and four kids came over and took the dog home with them.

"On their way out, Abe asked if they had any more dogs like that one and they said they had bought a male puppy when the bitch was missing. She invited us to stop and see him, and several weeks later we did. Abe and I couldn't believe our eyes when this male walked into the living room! He was great! He was about nine months old and, of course, not for sale.

"A couple of weeks later we called and asked if we could take him to an all-breed match, which they said was fine. Two matches later, Duke had won two Groups! When he was ten months old we asked if we could take him to a three-day circuit up in Fresno. The first two days he took his first points and went breed over five champions. The last day he went three out of three but the ring steward asked if she could buy him.

"It was at these shows that a gentleman with a Frenchie approached us about handling his dog. This turned out to be Ed Bigham, whose dog was a littermate of Duke…Ch. Joel of Balihai. We became close friends with Ed and his partner Bud Niles and spent many happy times with them. Duke finished soon after these shows and the owner allowed us to show him occasionally, but he still would not sell him to us.

"A big show weekend was coming up with a good Frenchie judge and we were enthused about showing Duke. The Thursday before the show, I called about

picking Duke up only to find out that he had run away. What? I placed an ad in the newspaper and finally received a phone call from a woman who had found Duke. We picked him up and took him home, and I called the owners and told them we had Duke and wanted to buy him. Several worrisome days later, she called back and said we could buy him for what they had paid for him—$200. The whole family came to say goodbye to Duke but he knew where his home was and didn't budge a foot beyond our front door."

Duke was Ch. Smith's Petit Maitre, bred by Robert Gephart and whelped in 1973. He lived to ten years of age. He sired 12 champions, including Best-in-Show winner Ch. Adams Traveling Man and Ch. Adams Unique Physique. Duke was the number-one Frenchie in 1975, 1976 and 1977, winning over 50 Bests of Breed each year. He won 16 Group Firsts in addition to being an all-breed Best in Show winner. He was known as a great showman with ears always erect and he had excellent movement. Suzi said, "He was easy to live with, very laid-back and loved to sleep in our bed under the covers. We dearly loved Duke and consider him our all-time favorite dog!"

The Jimmy Lee kennels of Foster Hanson in Texas were very active during the 1970s and 1980s. Not only did this kennel produce many champions but its dogs also provided the foundation stock for other kennels, including the Coxes' Goodtime dogs. Am./Mex. Ch. Jimmy Lee's Flip gained his American championship at the age of seven months and won a Best in Show at the age of eight months. Flip was sired by Ch. Hampton's Chevalier, a top producer, and out of Ch. Hampton's Mystique. He was pictured with his owner on the cover of the March 1974 *Dog World*.

And that brings us down the road of history to Herschel and Doris Cox, who surely made a major impact upon the breed. The Coxes were at a dog show, showing their English Bulldogs at the time, and fell in love with a Frenchie. They asked the Frenchie's owner if she was going to be bred. She was, and when the pups were five weeks old, the breeder called and said that she

Above: The Segals' Ch. Smith's Petit Maitre, "Duke."

had a puppy for them. The year was 1970 and from that time on, the Coxes moved forward with a breeding program that hadn't been seen before. In an interview with Herschel Cox by Jim Woodruff in the Winter 2002 *Just Frenchies* issue, Herschel noted, "There weren't that many Frenchies back when we started. It was hard to get one finished because they didn't have that many at the shows. There was one fella who was the stage manager down at the Grand Ol' Opry in Tennessee and we would find out which shows he was going to go to…When we sold a puppy, we would guarantee that they were healthy puppies and we would sell them as show quality. We were always very honest about our puppies and if they had a fault we would let the buyer know about it. We had no restriction on our puppies…if they wanted to show them they could, and if they wanted them as a pet, that was fine, too."

The foundation dog for the Coxes' Goodtime kennels was Ch. Scobey's Maurice Bon Homme, purchased at ten weeks of age from his breeder, Margaret Scobey. In 1979 the Coxes purchased two Fairmont dogs: Ch. Fairmont's Radar Ahead, sire of 13 champions including Ch. Mademoiselle Eve, top-producing Frenchie dam of all time; and Ch. Fairmont's Heart to Beat, sire of 23 champions. The list of winners from Goodtime kennels is impressive, and it would be impressive in any breed. Ch. Cox's Goodtime Charlie Brown sired 97 champions and is the top producer of French Bulldogs to date.

In the interview Herschel noted, "I think breed clubs are important to get breeders acquainted so they can compare notes on their breeding to improve the breed. So many people forget that the club is for the Frenchie and not for themselves." The Coxes and their Goodtime Frenchies left an impact on the breed that will be felt for many years.

In the late 1970s an article appeared in the *New York Times* with the headline: "24 French Bulldogs Set For Show in Plainfield" and went on to state that "…the 'Frenchie' is 100 in popularity in the AKC's popularity charts, but this is the status fanciers prefer to maintain." The East Coast turned out for this show, as it was the national specialty show of the FBDCA held in conjunction with the Plainfield Kennel Club's all-breed show. Helen Hover commented that this was a good

entry with real quality and was quoted in the aforementioned article: "There are currently only about 300 to 350 French Bulldogs in the United States. The policy of the club is not to breed excessively. The dogs are just bred for quality, not quantity. By breeding fewer, it's possible to be sure they arrive in good homes, where they are not commercialized." The author summed up the article with, "Obviously, it would be difficult to come up with an abandoned French Bulldog."

In the spring of 1979 Ed Bigham (Balihai kennels) wrote the following in the *Frenchie Fancier*: "Feb. 3rd and 4th, 1979, at the Golden Gate Show, the Frenchie Fanciers of the Western States held their SPECIAL of the year, marking the beginning of what is hoped to be a continuous yearly event for years to come. A total of 22 entries of very fine Frenchies were displayed for two days, benched amidst an array of satin blue, white and red bunting, white carpet, special name plates and a 24 by 4 foot mural painted in oil of a French Sidewalk Scene portraying French Bulldogs dressed as humans, doing their thing.

"Never in dog shows will a more compatible display of friendship, sportsmanship and good companionship be shown. Each person present, before, during and after the showing, was congenial, and congratulations were given to ALL winners, down to the very last. The warmth of the exhibitors and non-exhibitors alike will go down in history as one of the finest displays of co-operation ever portrayed at a Frenchie Special get-together."

STEPPING STONES TO THE 21ST CENTURY

The Growing Years—1980–1990

An energized era in the French Bulldog began with new and enthusiastic individuals coming to the fore. Young people, those with fresh ideas, brought their dreams and their dogs into the French Bulldog world, and it began to look as if the Frenchie would not be living out its life as a rare breed.

In 1980 registrations for the breed were at 170. Although small in number, the registrations had increased by almost 100 percent over the previous ten years. However, the 1981 national specialty saw an entry of only 12 Frenchies. Since 1933 the national specialty had been held as a part of an all-breed show, as entries were too low to support an independent show. From the first show on, the specialty had always been held on the East Coast even though for many years the majority of the breeders were living on the West Coast. In 1983, due to the efforts of three individuals, Colette Secher, Arlie Alford and Patti Adams, the FBDCA voted to rotate the location of the national specialties. The next year's specialty, held in Chicago, had a huge increase in entries over the previous years and, since that time, all national specialties have been rotated throughout the various regions of the country, with entries increasing each year. By the time of the club's centennial show in 1997 there were 303 dogs entered.

Colette Secher (formerly a breeder of Smooth Fox Terriers) of LeFox kennels met her first Frenchie in her early years in Paris. She collected whatever Frenchie memorabilia she could find and some years later started inquiring about a French Bulldog puppy. Helen Hover directed her to Gene and Patti Adams in California, who were doing some nice breeding. In their second litter Colette found the male that was to be the start of the LeFox Frenchies. Colette has bred good-looking, sound Frenchies, but probably the greatest to come out of her kennel was the multiple-Best-in-Show dog Ch. LeFox Goodtime Steel Magnolia, co-owned with Sarah Sweatt. Colette credits the many great Frenchies that have had a lasting impact upon the breed, but especially notes the Segals' Ch. Smith's Petit Maitre, Ch. Balihai's Quad, bred by Ed Bigham, and the dogs from the Terretts and from Janis Hampton.

McBeth's Frenchies were started in the early 1980s by Mark and Beth Carr. They purchased the four-year-old Ch. H and A's Top Hat And Tails ("Topper"); he contributed greatly to their breeding program and to others as well. Other key dogs in their breeding program were Ch. McBeth's Thunder LeBulRosewood, a top producer, and Ch. McBeth's T-Mann Le'Krislyn, who produced 18 champions. In addition to winning Groups, he loved attention and loved to get his way! Ch.

McBeth's Tail Gator was a Best in Show dog and the number-one French Bulldog in 1999 and 2000, the first Pied to achieve this honor. Ch. H and A's Fleur D'Amour, sired by Topper, was the top-producing female in 1993. Ch. McBeth's Lizz Taylor, out of Thunder, was the top-producing female in 1997. Upon her retirement she became a therapy dog and helped patients during chemotherapy sessions. Beth said that by the end of 2005 they had produced their 100th Frenchie titleholder. It's also quite an accomplishment that Mark and Beth's dogs are breeder-owner-handled.

Luis and Patty Sosa have been breeding Frenchies under the Bandog prefix since the 1980s. The key dogs in their breeding program have been Ch. Balihai's Quad, Ch. Adams Unique Physique and Ch. Bandog's One In A Million. Their biggest winners have been Ch. Bandog's Earnin' Respect, with 11 Bests in Show and three national specialty wins, and Ch. Bandog's Jump for Joy, with 20 all-breed Bests in Show and one national specialty win. Their dogs have won five FBDCA national specialties and 34 all-breed Bests in Show at the time of this writing, and Ch. Bandog's Jump for Joy was the number-one Non-Sporting dog in 2004, the first Frenchie to achieve this since Ch. Ralanda Ami Francine in 1964. Four all-breed Bests in Show and three national specialties were owner-handled.

Carol and Richard Meyer of Starhaven kennels began their Frenchie breeding in 1987. The key dog in their breeding program was Ch. Enstrom's El Bee Great, a top producer with 23 champions to his credit. Their Ch. Fisher's Mon Reve of Starhaven was Best of Breed at the 1989 Purina Invitational and Group Three, and Best of Opposite Sex at the 1988 national specialty. Ch. Vi Du Lac Starhaven's Hot Flash, a Best in Show dog, and Ch. Vi Du Lac Starhaven's Dante were all good winners. Many champions have come out of the Starhaven kennels, and the Meyers are still active in the breed.

Dorit Fischler DVM of Belboulecan kennels in Ontario, Canada began her Frenchie life in 1989 and has bred some lovely Frenchies. The dogs that have

Facing page, top: "Thunder's" first Best in Show: Ch. McBeth's Thunder LeBulRosewood with breeder-owner-handler Beth Carr.
Facing page, bottom: A Best in Show-winning dog from Starhaven, Ch. Vi Du Lac Starhaven's Hot Flash.

added the most to her breeding program have been Belboulecan Histoire De Ma Vie, Belboulecan Hungaria ZsaZsa and Belboulecan Lady Dragon Fly. Can./Am. Ch. Platinum Belboulecan Babalou was Best of Winners at the FBDCA centennial specialty at 12 months of age; the following day she went Best of Breed and Group One at the supported entry at the all-breed show. She gained her American championship in the first three days she was shown in the US and also won an Award of Merit at the 1999 national specialty. Can./Am. Ch. Belboulecan Hungaria ZsaZsa was Best of Winners at the 1999 FBDCA national and Best of Opposite Sex to her son at the supported entry of the 2000 FBDCA specialty. Can./Am. Ch. Belboulecan Lady Dragon Fly was the number-one Frenchie in Canada in 1995. Dorit is still very active in the breed and attends the FBDCA national specialties when they are not too far from her Canadian residence.

Bob and Laura Condon have also had Frenchies since 1989 and do limited breeding under the Colby prefix. Laura says, "We saw some Frenchies at a show and fell in love with the breed. A few months later it was love at first sight when we met Roo, Ch. Excel's Rowdy Too of Colby, our first French Bulldog. Since then we have had a great time breeding and showing our wonderful Frenchies. In 2005 Ch. Colby's Divine Design was number-one Frenchie bitch and Best of Breed at Westminster Kennel Club. Millie is a sweet little girl who loves to show and is a pleasure to live with. We always look forward to seeing what the next generation brings!"

There were many more breeders in the 1980s who bear mentioning: Rick and Michelle Shannon of Smokey Valley kennels; Luca Carbone of Jaguar kennels; Judy Enstrom of Enstrom's kennels; Al and Enid Hendricks of Flim Flam kennels; Gene and Patti Adams of Adams kennels; and Arlie Alford of LeBull kennels. All have been strong supporters of the breed, breeding winning and top-producing animals.

The Beginnings of Popularity—The 1990s

The breed was now gaining in popularity with each decade. By the 1990s the French Bulldog was around 85th in popularity among the AKC-recognized breeds,

with registrations for the year 1990 at 632, an increase of 462 over the 170 dogs registered in 1980. New breeders and exhibitors were coming to the fore and Frenchies were winning more Groups at the shows. The breed also was becoming more familiar to the public. The years of being considered a "rare breed" were waning.

Robin Millican started breeding Frenchies in 1990 and has produced a number of Frenchie champions. She considers Ch. Kobi's Victor and Ch. Fourstars Lucky

Lady to be the key dogs in her breeding program. Ch. Kobi's On The Marc, sire of 13 champions, was the number-one owner-handled Frenchie in 1998. Victor won the Breed in 2001 at the AKC/Eukanuba show, received first Award of Merit at the AKC/Eukanuba show in 2002 and was Best of Opposite Sex at the 2002 national specialty in Portland, Oregon.

Shauna Ann Woodruff, Shann's French Bulldogs, whelped her first litter in 1993. The key dog in her breeding program has been Ch. Spicewood's Mr. Bojangles, sire of 17 champions. She notes, "Not only is Mr. Bojangles an exceptionally well bred dog, he is also extremely healthy and has a sound, sweet-natured temperament, even at 12 years of age!" Exceptional wins of the Shann's dogs have been Best in Sweepstakes at the 1999 FBDCA national specialty, the number-one bitch in the United States in 2002, Best of Breed at Westminster in 2003 and Best of Breed at the national specialty in 2005. Over 40 champions, in addition to multiple Group winners, have come out of this kennel.

Kathy Dannel Vitcak of Jackpot! French Bulldogs certainly was a force to be reckoned with in the 1990s. Kathy fell in love with the breed in the early 1990s while living in Texas. She considers Ch. Jackpot! Kwik Pik Tiket Petty, bred by Cheryl Petty, to be her foundation bitch. Bred to Ch. Cox's Goodtime Charlie Brown, she produced Ch. Jackpot! Ez Come…Ez Go, a top-winning Frenchie and a top-producing sire. EZ went to live in Holland with Frenchie breeder Arja de Boer, where he has continued his wins in Europe from the Veteran Class. Ch. Jackpot! Diva Las Vegas, a littermate to EZ, was a Pedigree top-producing bitch and the dam of Ch. Jackpot! Money, Money, Money CGC, ROM. Money was the first French Bulldog to be awarded a CHIC (Canine Health Information Center) certification. Money has sired 22 champions, including the first Orthopedic Foundation for Animals (OFA) Excellent French Bulldog, Ch. Jackpot! For The Love Of Money. The exceptional dog from this kennel was Ch. Jackpot! I'm the Boss of JustUs, bred by Kathy and owned by

Ron and Suzanne Readmond . He was the top-winning Frenchie in the show ring in 2003 and 2004.

Kathy wrote, "The Jackpot! kennel name came to me as a result of how I felt when I discovered the world of purebred dogs —like I had hit the Jackpot! Top wins and honors were fun when they happened, but I must say the biggest thrill comes from the many true and enduring friendships I have made through French Bulldogs."

James Dalton and his Fabelhaft kennels are now located in the rolling hills of southern Ohio. Fabelhaft was established in Ireland by James in 1974, when his parents bought him a Smooth Dachshund as a birthday gift. Although that first dog was not a success in the show ring, it sparked a competitive interest in the breeding and exhibition of purebred dogs that remains a passion at Fabelhaft to this day. James won his first Best in Show with a Smooth Dachshund bitch at the age of 16 and that same year became the youngest person to judge the breed in Ireland. Throughout his teenage years James continued to build the Fabelhaft name, breeding and exhibiting several Best in Show and multi-Group-winning Dachshunds in addition to acquiring his first Afghan Hound.

By the mid-1980s James had earned a degree in fashion design from the Royal College of Art in London, relocated to the United States and successfully pursued his career. In 1993 James and his partner, Dr. John Turjoman, reestablished their interest in dogs and had much success in exhibiting and breeding Afghan Hounds. James wrote, "I decided it might be fun to have a 'wash and wear' companion for the Afghans and by chance at a dog show in 1996 I met Ann McCammon of Justamere fame, who had a six-month-old fawn male puppy, 'Duggan,' who I immediately fell in love with and literally begged Ann to sell him to me! This dog, Ch. Justamere's Dunkin F'R Apples, at just 11 months old, became the number-one French Bulldog in the nation in 1997, handled by myself and co-owned with Ann. I later purchased a half-brother, Ch. Justamere's

Facing page, top: Ch. Colby's Divine Design at Westminster.
Facing page, bottom: Ch. Fabelhaft Majic Marc-R is a top producer for Fabelhaft and multi-Group winner, among his many achievements.

Golden Budha of Fabelhaft, who has contributed greatly to our breeding program.

"John and I have continued to successfully build the Fabelhaft line, producing several top specials including Ch. Fabelhaft Majic Marc-R; Ch. Fabelhaft Flower Power, dam of nine champions including current top-winning Best-in-Show dog Ch. Fabelhaft Too Hot To Handle; and the Group-winning brothers Ch. Fabelhaft X-Marcs The Spot and Ch. Fabelhaft King Louis.

"In 2001, upon meeting Canadian fanciers Dr. Kim and Shelley St. John of Robobull kennel, who were also building their Frenchie line, we formed a unique friendship and partnership. The four of us share a love of the breed and demand the very best in our breeding programs. Shelley and I have combined our passion to produce some of the top-winning dogs of the decade, including the record-breaking multiple Best in Show Am./Can. Ch. Robobull Fabelhaft Inferno, 'Dante,' the number-one French Bulldog all-systems in the USA for 2005. His son, Best in Show Am./Can. Ch. Fabelhaft

Too Hot To Handle, 'Tony,' owned by Dr. David and Jill Neidig, is currently the number-one French Bulldog all-systems in the USA for 2006. Dante is currently the number-one French Bulldog in Canada for 2006."

In just ten years the Fabelhaft kennels have owned and/or bred three number-one French Bulldogs. Their philosophy, as well as that of the St. Johns, has always been that French Bulldogs are companions first and show dogs second. The future, indeed, looks very bright for these two kennels.

Many individuals were breeding lovely winning Fenchies during the 1990s. Mention should be made of the following breeders and kennels: Kristyne Affeldt of Affabulls kennels bred Ch. Affabulls King of Diamonds, a top producer with 29 champions to his credit. Trudy Bettinger of TeaD's and Bullistik kennels bred many champions. Leota and Kenneth Bannister of Kenle kennels and Mike Loller of Legacy were all active and busy in the whelping box as well as in the show ring. Joyce Haas of Hedgebrook kennels has not only bred a number of champions but also has been the president of the FBDCA for several years, leading the club through many problems that a breed, which is gaining rapidly in popularity, can experience. Nanette Goldberg of Marionette kennels was a colorful breeder in the decade and produced a number of winning Frenchies, including Ch. Blazin Bull-Marc-It, winner of the national specialty in 1994 and Best of Breed two times at the Westminster show.

The Frenchie can sit back, relax and enjoy the devotion of its fanciers.

9

The Frenchie
RÉVOLUTION

2000–

Only time will tell who the future breeders of fine French Bulldogs will be. But the beginning of the 21st century sees a number of individuals who are breeding champions and are active in the show ring.

Teresa Bjork of Des Moines, Iowa purchased her first Frenchie in 2000 from the Pudgybull kennel of Marilyn Burdick, a longtime well-known Bulldog breeder. Like many, Teresa and her family increased their number of Frenchies; their three include Ch. Pudgybull Crème Brulee, called "Bruster." Teresa says, "Bruster is our little champion and our first show dog. My husband Craig went to our local training class and learned the basics and then we traveled to the shows and learned the rest by just doing it! We have had a lot of fun and we adore our little Frenchie clown, as he makes us laugh and smile. He has a beret that he wears after he's been shown. He sits on my lap in the car, just as big as you please! We call it his victory hat. He takes it very seriously and loves it when I put the hat on him, smiling from ear to ear, so proud of himself!" The next in line is their young Pudgybull Petite Fleur Babette. Teresa also notes that "our Frenchies are loved and adored. We have made many friends from the shows and we enjoy seeing them as we travel around."

Sandy Plotts of Le Jardin kennels had her first litter in 2003 and credits the guidance of experienced Frenchie breeders in helping her to be able to produce some very nice Frenchies. The key dog in her breeding program is Ch. Petite Cherie's Rosebud CGC, TDI, called "Rosie." Rosie loved to be shown, and she produced two litters from which five champions came. Rosie won an Award of Merit at the 2004 FBDCA specialty show in Texas. Sandy writes, "She is the queen of the house and rules the other Frenchies with a firm hand. She has always been a joy to own and is very special to us."

Nancy and Michael Magill own Ch. Hedgebrooks 'Tis Himself, bred by Sharon Trotter and Joyce Haas. Born in 2004, "Maestro" gained his Canadian championship,

dog was the best! Maestro's first real show was a disaster, as I was so nervous I forgot to take the bait out of my pocket and he was very busy finding bait all over the floor. His little nose never left the floor while I walked around the ring saying, 'Leave it, leave it, leave it,' constantly jerking his lead. I left the ring a complete wreck, never wanting to return.

"Meeting other show people is how the novice learns. I found everyone was willing to share their experiences, advice, tips, tricks and evaluations. I would talk and listen to anyone and everyone, like a sponge absorbing as much information as I could on grooming, handling, etc. The challenge in showing is what makes it fun."

Nancy continues, "Maestro is a flirt, he truly loves women, both human and dogs. He loves the Bulldog he lives with, and it is fun to watch him run up and bite her on the butt or back of the leg, then run like hell. He is forever trying to put the moves on her. The

along with a Group One, at the age of eight months. He finished his American championship at one year of age, with four majors and two Bests of Breed. In six months he won over 40 Bests of Breed and placed in the Group one-third of the time, including multiple Group Firsts. Maestro excels in structure, balance and movement. Nancy writes, "His favorite things to do are to run wild through the house for no apparent reason, bait the house Bulldog in a game of chase, which he always wins, eat popsicles and go absolutely crazy every time he sees a rabbit in the yard!"

For those new to showing, Nancy has written well about the experience of being a newcomer to the ring. "Our first show was a fun match and Maestro was four months old. We won our Group and then we won Best in Match. Imagine the glory of owning your first show dog, handling him yourself at your first show and winning Best in Show! I was hooked! Our

Above, top: Ch. Pudgybull Sugar and Spice, "Ginger."
Above, bottom: Ch. Pudgybull Crème Brulee, "Bruster," donning his "victory hat."
Facing page, top: Ch. Le Jardin's Spruce It Up, "Spruce," is a son of Le Jardin kennels' important bitch Rosie.
Facing page, bottom: Ch. Bon Marv's EZ As Pied Jackpot! CGC, TDI, RN, CD, ROM.

Bulldog has a good 40 pounds on him, but he seems to know all the right moves to dodge her and he will run under or through things that she can't fit through."

Probably among the most active in the show ring in the new millennium have been Suzanne and Ron Readmond of JustUs kennels. Suzanne wrote, "I have been involved with dogs most of my life but always as a terrier fancier. Frenchies caught my eye at the dog shows and I began to learn about the breed, deciding early on that I really needed a good Frenchie. Lucky for me, 'Spenser Adam' entered my life in 2000 (Ch. Jackpot! Money Is Everything CGC), a birthday gift from my husband, Ron. The love affair was on as Ron fell victim to the lure of Frenchies and Spenser was soon joined by 'Savannah Lee' (Ch. Jackpot! Money Is the Only Thing).

"Savannah Lee was to be our foundation bitch and we bred her to the dog I co-owned, and now own, Ch. Bon Marv's EZ As Pied Jackpot! CGC, TDI, RN, CD, ROM, bred by Marv Simonson. The resulting litter of three, our first litter, all became champions under the JustUs kennel name. We then began a breeder relationship and bred under the JustJackpot and JustUs names. 'GP' (Ch. Jackpot! I'm The Boss

of JustUs) was purchased from his breeder in January 2002 and became our shining star in the ring. He was number-one Frenchie in 2003 and 2004. While he was 'on the road' we chose to keep him busy in the show ring and he is now making his mark as a stud dog. We feel that GP will shine far into the future and we hope that we, as breeders, will be remembered as caring properly for the lines that brought him to us and the lines with which he has been mated.

"We gave our kennel the JustUs name as both Ron and I have grown children and so it is 'just us' in this endeavor. We feel we are truly a kennel of the 21st century and plan on joining the breeders who are breeding and raising healthy, happy and sound Frenchies.

"In 2002 we began publishing the *JustFrenchies* magazine as a way to share our love of the breed with others. We felt we wanted to give something back to the breed that has brought us, in such a short time, so much happiness. Through the magazine we have gained many new friends and with each issue we have learned more and more about the Frenchie and his world.

"If we were to reflect upon who we are and where we are going, we began with Frenchies primarily as the show part of a partnership, but love of the breed

The French Bulldog

30 and 40 years ago. It takes several generations of breeding, as well as time, before the dogs who have made an impact upon the breed can be seen. A string of Bests in Show make a great dog, but if this dog becomes a top producer, and in turn has sons or daughters who become top producers, you find the dogs who are the cornerstones of the breed.

Although the Frenchie was considered a rare breed for many years, the dogs and breeders who have made a difference stand out. The French Bulldog has, indeed, been fortunate to have had the Terretts, Janis Hampton and Herschel and Doris Cox, who have made a profound and lasting contribution to the betterment of the Frenchie. It always takes perseverance, dedication and tolerance to last over the decades and to continue to breed healthy, beautiful Frenchies.

In 1985 registrations were at 318 for the year. By 1995 they had increased to 1039. Record registrations were reached in 2005, when the breed placed 38th in popularity among the AKC breeds, with registrations at 4,210.

Time will tell whether this popularity will last, but the conventional wisdom says that the breed will settle down with a drop in popularity. The French Bulldog is not the breed for everyone. His health problems, his care and his personality make him unique, and he must have owners who recognize this uniqueness.

In the meantime, the responsibility for keeping the French Bulldog healthy and a viable breed falls, as always, upon the French Bull Dog Club of America and the responsible breeders. This is the organization and the individuals who have taken the breed to heart and are breeding and showing outstanding, healthy and personable dogs. In turn, these are the breeders who will see that the Frenchie remains in good hands and that the breed will remain a great one for years to come.

and a desire to make a difference has refocused us. We look forward to seeing many JustUs-bred puppies in the ring for generations to come."

Others active in the show ring in this century have been Karen Cram with Ch. Karendon's Igor Die Fledermaus and Bob and Laura Condon of Colby kennels with Ch. Colby's Divine Design, Best of Breed at Westminster Kennel Club in 2005. Two top winners in 2006 who have appeared consistently in the top rankings for the breed are Ch. Fabelhaft Too Hot To Handle, owned by Dr. David and Jill Neidig, and Ch. Daulokke's Nordique Crouton, owned by Donna Cron, Kathy Manylech and James Dalton. Ch. Etoile Billy Joe Royal, owned by Catherine Crislip and Claire Johnson, is a multiple-Group-winning Frenchie from Texas. Another Group-winning Frenchie is Ch. Celestial Whereforarthou, owned by Dr. and Mrs. Mandetta and Casey Fletcher.

In all breeds it is easier to go to the past, looking into the records and pedigrees of dogs who were active

Above: Multiple Best in Show and 2006 FBDCA national specialty winner Ch. Fabelhaft Too Hot To Handle.
Facing page, top: An American and Canadian champion by one year of age and a dapper dresser to boot is Ch. Hedgebrooks 'Tis Himself.
Facing page, bottom: A big winner of the 21st century is Ch. Bandog's Jump for Joy, the number-one Frenchie for 2004. Pictured with handler Larry Cornelius.

PART IV
FRENCHIE ROYALS & ARISTOCRATS

Chicago, 1986: Regina D'Orage de McKee CDX (LEFT) and La Petite Pierrot de McKee UD, looking out the window at the Blackstone Hotel during the first independent FBDCA specialty.

10

Meet the
PARENT
Club

By James Grebe

THE BEGINNINGS OF THE FBDCA

French Bulldogs were first exhibited at Westminster in 1896, and the following year the breed was featured on the cover of the 1897 Westminster catalog even though it was not yet an AKC-approved breed. At that time, British and French breeders strongly favored the rose ear, and there was no published standard for French Bulldogs in France, England or anywhere else in Europe. Both bat-eared and rose-eared dogs were exhibited at that show, but the English judge George Raper put up only the rose-eared ones, which infuriated the American fanciers, who preferred the bat ear. They were so incensed that on April 5, 1897, American breeders met at the famous Delmonico's Restaurant in New York where they formed the French Bull Dog Club of America (FBDCA) and adopted a breed standard allowing only the bat ear.

Thus the FBDCA was the first breed club anywhere in the world dedicated solely to the French Bulldog. According to the 1926 book *The French Bulldog*, the FBDCA breed standard "…was the first authoritative declaration, by any organized body, clearly defining the qualities that should characterize French bulldogs." The first elected officers of the FBDCA were Walter W. Watrous, president; George N. Phelps, vice president; Richard H. Hunt, treasurer; and John R. Buchan, secretary. All 20 of the charter members were, of course, men, since in those times women did not even show their own dogs in public venues. Along with promoting the bat ear, the FBDCA was also discouraging the crossing of Boston Terriers with Frenchies, which was a problem at that time. The club also began withholding support and trophies for judges who were not following the club's breed standard.

The next year at the 1898 Westminster show, the American fanciers were so outraged when they learned that there were to be classes for both bat-eared and rose-eared dogs that they immediately pulled their dogs and the American judge refused to participate in the show. The year-old French Bull Dog Club of America organized its own show, for bat-eared dogs only, to be held at the luxurious Waldorf-Astoria hotel. This was the famous first specialty of the FBDCA, which, incidentally, was the first dog show ever to be held in a hotel.

THE FIRST SPECIALTY

As reported in *The French Bulldog*, "It was the first time in the history of American dogs that a show had ever been held amid such luxurious surroundings as the Waldorf-Astoria afforded, while the high social character of those who stood back of the enterprise made the event one that prominent society people very generally patronized…Several hundred finely engraved cards of invitation were sent out and the day of the show the room in the Waldorf-Astoria was thronged with an enthusiastic crowd of admirers and supporters of the breed." Forty-six Frenchies were entered in this first specialty: 26 dogs and 20 bitches. A brindle dog named Dimboolaa, owned by Amy C. Gillig, was chosen Best of Breed.

Here is how the February 13, 1898 issue of the *New York Herald* (whose owner was an honorary member of the FBDCA) described the occasion:

"Never was a bench show held within so sumptuous an environment as that of the French Bulldog Club held at the Waldorf-Astoria yesterday afternoon and evening. Far up in the sun parlor, on the topmost floor of the building, amid palms and potted plants and rich rugs and soft divans, fifty bulldogs were on exhibition.

"The French bulldog has but lately come into prominence, but already it has attained the rank of a principal favorite of society, and on the seat of many a carriage whirling up Fifth Avenue or through Central Park, the funny-faced bulldogs may be seen beside richly dressed ladies, who frequently pet and caress them."

"After the dogs (were shown), of course, society came in for a share of the attraction. Pretty nearly everybody was there. A striking feature was the entrance of prominent ladies into the ring, to display their pet dogs before the judges. This innovation was possible because of the semi-private character of the exhibition."

THE EARLY YEARS

In the early part of the 20th century, most members of the FBDCA lived in the New York area, so monthly club meetings were held there along with an annual dinner meeting held at a hotel. The club membership in those days included such luminaries as a Belmont, a Whitney, a Roosevelt and assorted Vanderbilts, along with honorary members Elsie de Wolfe (a very colorful character often credited with inventing the profession of interior decorating, and a woman far ahead of her time) and James Gordon Bennett. Bennett owned the *New York Herald* newspaper, and it was he who sent the reporter Stanley to Africa to search for Dr. David Livingstone; he was also commodore of the New York Yacht club.

Following the over-the-top first national specialty show in 1898, the club held no more specialties until 1910, although it did support shows by offering valuable trophies whenever Frenchies were shown under its regularly appointed judges. In 1910 the club held its second specialty, at which 127 Frenchies were shown. From then on, national specialties were held annually; the first quarter of the 20th century was a very active time for the club and the breed in several regards.

In 1911 the FBDCA endorsed the French Bulldog Club of New England to be a member of the AKC. Later on, the Chicago-based Western French Bulldog Club also joined the AKC with the parent club's approval. The following year's specialty was held on April 20, 1912, just six days after the sinking of the *Titanic*. One of the three-judge panel for the specialty was Samuel Goldenberg, who had boarded the *Titanic* in Cherbourg in order to get to New York in time to judge at the specialty. (In 1904 Goldenberg had imported from France a young Frenchie named Nellcote Gamin, described in *The French Bulldog* as "the main pillar in the establishment of French Bulldogs in America.") Goldenberg had judged the 1911 specialty and drew the

Facing page: An FBDCA special ribbon from 1915.

largest French Bulldog entry of any show ever held in the world up to that date. Remarkably, when the *Titanic* went down, Samuel and his wife both survived; they arrived in New York City on April 18, giving him just one full day to recuperate before judging at the specialty. Though specialties are often fraught with some sort of high drama, that remains probably the most dramatic judging assignment in the club's history.

As a sidebar, while speaking of the *Titanic*, there were a number of dogs on the ill-fated ship when it left Southhamptom, England in April of 1912. Mr. Robert Daniels was traveling with his French Bulldog Fr. Ch. Gamin De Pycombe, whom he had purchased in France. Although Mr. Daniels survived the disaster, his unfortunate French Bulldog did not. However, being an astute businessman, Mr. Daniels had had his Frenchie insured for $750 and this claim was presented for payment to the insurance company.

The year 1913 was most notable for the publication of an unofficial monthly magazine titled *The French Bull Dog*, published by club members. However, it was discontinued due to finances after only nine issues, as revenues from circulation and advertising covered only about one-fourth of the total costs (a year's subscription was only $1.50, postage included). Anyone lucky enough to find even a single issue of the magazine today, in any condition, must be prepared to pay a princely sum for it.

The 1910 through 1913 specialties were all held at the lavish Hotel Astor in New York City. If out-of-town exhibitors could not attend, they could ship their dogs to the hotel, where a committee of the club would care for them. The 1913 specialty, held in April in the Astor Hotel's rooftop glass-enclosed Belvedere Club, was described as having "a sun parlor, bepotted and bepalmed," which opened up to a roof garden with bushes and shrubs for exercising the dogs. Inside the ring was a large raised dais covered with olive cotton duck cloth, where the 135 entered dogs were shown. In that year, a Produce Stakes was held in conjunction with the specialty and 30 nominated bitches (who could be nominated up to one week prior to whelping date) competed for a $400 purse, a considerable sum in 1913. During this period the prizes at shows included silver cups as well as cash; a particularly nice trophy was a Reed

and Barton pewter tankard with the original club medallion, designed by renowned artist and sculptor Marguerite Kirmse, attached.

In 1916, John E. Haslam was elected FBDCA president and served in that office for 20 years, until 1936, a remarkable achievement and one which no doubt required considerable stamina and patience.

The club's fundraising in those early days often included selling raffle tickets at specialties, with a puppy as a prize; imagine the outcry if this were done today. However, this must have been a rather successful way to raise money, as the club was able to support charitable causes. In 1923–1925, the FBDCA donated $7,000 to an orphanage in Yonkers, New York.

In 1925, at which time the club had 86 active members, the FBDCA, along with the French Bulldog Club of New England, underwrote the milestone book *The French Bulldog* ("the blue book"), which upon publication in 1926 sold for $5 per copy. Almost 15 years later in 1940, the club offered the unsold copies at a special price of $3 each, but in 1954 the price went back up to $5! This book, which today is considered a rare find and commands very high prices, contained articles from the 1913 magazine *The French Bull Dog*. These dealt with breed history, information on French Bulldog breeding in Europe and the American breed standard; it also included drawings that are still widely reprinted today.

THE DEPRESSION YEARS

Like everyone else, French Bulldog fanciers felt the financial crunch of the Great Depression of the 1930s. However, they persevered and were able to keep the club alive, albeit with fewer members and in reduced circumstances. The FBDCA would have been unable to hold its 1931 specialty had not a last-minute canvass of members managed to raise enough money to cover the show expenses. The judge was asked to serve without fee. At the end of 1933 there were only 38 club members, and in 1936 only 32. However, membership increased when the initiation fee was waived. In 1933, the specialty was held in conjunction with the Morris and Essex show, and this continued to be the case through 1941. The 1939 show had an entry of 100 Frenchies, which was the largest entry in many years.

THE WAR YEARS

"Mention should also be made of the conditions confronting this country due to the European war. What effect this will have on us, no one can foretell, but in the 44 years of its existence, the French Bull Dog Club of America has weathered many depressions and one world war, and it is up to every member to do all in his or her power to assist the club in every way possible during these times of uncertainty."—FBDCA Secretary's Annual Report for 1940.

From 1942 through 1947 the specialties were held in conjunction with the Westchester Kennel Club instead of Morris and Essex, and the entries for wartime specialties averaged fewer than 50 Frenchies. Still, the breed and breed clubs fared better in America than in war-torn Europe, where the situation was grim indeed for dogs as well as for people.

THE POST-WAR PERIOD

The 1948 specialty was held in conjunction with the Kennel Club of Northern New Jersey's show. Although over half of the club members lived outside the eastern area, the club rejected the idea of appointing club representatives in various parts of the country in order to increase membership. Club officers and executive committee members continued to be those members who lived in the New York City area and usually met four to six times per year. During the presidency of Fred Hamm (1937–1951), many of those meetings were held at the Advertising Club in Manhattan, as Hamm was manager of the General Outdoor Advertising Co. in New York. In 1949 the specialty went back to the Westchester Kennel Club in Rye, New York, where it was held annually through 1956.

MID-CENTURY

In 1950 there were 47 FBDCA members and 31 entries at the specialty. In 1951 the club rejected a change to the standard, proposed by the Pacific Coast French Bulldog Club, that would have allowed the color black. The club also rejected a proposal to raise the weight limit. It did, however, approve the Midwest French Bulldog Club's proposal that the specialty include an open class for whites, creams, fawns and pieds, evidence of the growing popularity of these colors in the early 1950s.

In 1952 the FBDCA voted to approve an amendment to AKC rules that would allow women to serve as AKC delegates; however, no female AKC delegates were

Above and facing page: This mural belongs to the FBDCA and depicts Frenchies in a French sidewalk scene. It measures 24 feet by 4 feet and is displayed annually at the FBDCA national specialty.

seated until 1974. In 1953 the club had only 40 members and 33 entries at the specialty.

The club eliminated the two Open Classes under 17 pounds for the 1954 specialty. The following year, 1955, Helen Hover became FBDCA secretary, succeeding longtime secretary Evelyn Halsey, and began publishing several club bulletins per year. Helen was to serve as secretary for an astonishing 30 years, an achievement unlikely ever to be equaled. The 1957 through 1966 specialties returned to the site of the 1948 show, the Kennel Club of Northern New Jersey in Teaneck, New Jersey. In 1958 the FBDCA denied permission for the Pacific Coast French Bulldog Club to become an AKC member. Throughout the 1950s and 1960s there were usually three or four club meetings per year, usually with fewer than a dozen attending, at a New York City hotel or the home of a member.

THE 1960s AND 1970s

As copies of *The French Bulldog* were becoming scarce, it was voted in 1964 to sell copies only to members for their own use. In 1967 the specialty was moved to the Trenton Kennel Club show in Trenton, New Jersey, with only 18 Frenchies entered. The specialty would remain in Trenton for ten years, through 1976. Club membership in 1967 was up to 54, and by 1970 had jumped to 95 club members with 44 Frenchies in 79 total entries at the specialty, the largest specialty since 1948.

During the 1960s and '70s there were unsuccessful attempts to interest the club's board in holding the specialty outside the New York/New Jersey area. In 1975 it was decided that although a club member could receive the club's annual financial statement on request, these statements would not be regularly sent out to the membership. In another change in policy, it was decided

that membership lists would be given out to members.

From 1977 until 1981, Marilyn Dockstader in Illinois published a magazine called *The Frenchie Fancier*, an endeavor that the FBDCA board initially discouraged. During the same period, from 1977 through 1983, the annual specialties were held in conjunction with the Plainfield (New Jersey) Kennel Club shows. Around this time the FBDCA board considered reprinting *The French Bulldog* but decided that the project would be too expensive (it would have cost $11–13 for each exact-sized copy). A member appealed to the club to set up some sort of structure to promote the welfare of French Bulldogs "in trouble, lost, strayed or in poor surroundings," but this appeal was rejected by the club in 1978. That same year there were only 20 Frenchies entered in the specialty, with supported shows in the West and the Midwest. By this year, club membership had increased to 106.

THE 1980s AND 1990s

During the 1980s the FBDCA became a truly national club and began holding national specialties outside the East Coast region. During these years, the club also began involvement in rescue activities, education and health and genetics. The membership began to grow, as did the club's finances. Though *The Frenchie Fancier* ceased publication in 1981, the following year Arlie Alford (at that time McCoy) of Minnesota began publishing another independent breed magazine, *The French Bullytin*.

The 1984 specialty, the first ever held outside the New York/New Jersey area, was held in Chicago in conjunction with the International Kennel Club. At that landmark event there was an exhibit of Frenchie art and collectibles, a photo exhibit, a commemorative plate by

Linda McKee and a banquet that featured chocolate French Bulldogs made from an antique mold. That same year, Helen Hover retired as FBDCA secretary after her 30 years of service. The following year, 1985, the specialty returned to the East Coast and was at the Plainfield Kennel Club show, with the Futurity Produce stakes being replaced by a Sweepstakes. The 1986 specialty returned to the Midwest, being held at the Edwardsville (Illinois) Kennel Club show; the same year, Frank Meyer succeeded Peggy Clark Kelly as president, following her 14-year tenure.

The next two years saw independent specialties held in Chicago again at the combined specialties shows. In 1987 three board members were elected from outside the East Coast, the first time this had happened in many years. As a consequence, the board began meeting via teleconference calls rather than in person. By 1988 the club had 143 members, and that year a genetics committee was formed, the name of which was later changed to health and genetics committee. The following year of 1989 saw many changes, as Brenda Buckles and Nancy Makinen began the process of developing a club rescue commitee and program at the specialty in San Rafael, California. The constitution and by-laws were amended to allow for two-year terms for officers and directors, and club recognition of local/regional clubs was established. The Frenchie Fanciers of Mid-Florida became the first regional club to apply for such recognition. A new code of ethics was adopted. And as a sad note to end the decade, Dick Hover, AKC delegate from 1953–1989, died, ending an era.

The 1990s saw much club activity in the areas of breed rescue, education of breeders and judges, health surveys, involvement of the club with the AKC Canine Health Foundation and geographically dispersed specialties. By the 1990 specialty in Minneapolis, Minnesota the club had changed from having an executive committee to a board of directors. The breed standard (which had been unchanged since 1947) was revised to conform with the AKC format. The next year at the 1991 specialty in New Orleans, the AKC French Bulldog breed video was brought out to great acclaim. The specialty in 1992 was in Anaheim, California, and during that same year the results of the club's first health survey were published.

The 1993, '94, and '95 specialties were in Allentown, Pennsylvania; Orlando, Florida; and Sacramento, California, respectively, with the membership at the Sacramento show voting to have the club donate money to the newly formed AKC Canine Health Foundation. The 1996 specialty in Plano, Texas, had for the first time a web page, being hosted on Carol Taylor's web site. The following year of 1997 was the club's centennial specialty, marking 100 years since the founding of the FBDCA. The centennial show was held in Overland Park, Kansas and had a record entry of 303 dogs with 429 total entries competing in obedience, Sweepstakes, Junior Showmanship and conformation. Several foreign dogs were entered and there were many foreign visitors in attendance, as our club was the first club in the world dedicated exclusively to French Bulldogs, and therefore was the first to observe its centenary. It was generally agreed that this special show was a fitting tribute to the French Bull Dog Club of America's first century.

THE SECOND CENTURY BEGINS

Advances around the end of the twentieth century included publication of the Illustrated Standard in 1997, establishment of a French Bulldog Donor Advised Fund with the Canine Health Foundation, participation in the AKC Parent Club DNA program, establishment of a club web site at www.frenchbulldog club.org and establishment of a Registry of Merit. The specialties from 1998 through 2007 were held in widely dispersed venues: Sacramento, California; Minneapolis, Minnesota; Buffalo, New York; Beaverton, Oregon; Salt Lake City, Utah; Indianapolis, Indiana; Arlington, Texas; Sacramento, California; Gatlinburg, Tennessee; and Denver, Colorado. During those years, club membership and show entries steadily climbed as the breed became more and more popular. It is hoped that the second century of the club and the breed in America will surpass the achievements of the first century.

Facing page: The cover of the 1897 Westminster Kennel Club catalog, on which a French Bulldog is featured.

WESTMINSTER
KENNEL CLUB
21st Annual
Dog Show
1897
FEB'Y. 22, 23, 24, 25
MADISON SQUARE GARDEN

A rear view of Ch. Bon Marv's EZ as Pied Jackpot! shows strong and muscular hind legs that are longer than the front legs so that the loin is elevated above the shoulders.

11

On
JUDGING
the French Bulldog

By Virginia Rowland
Chair, Judges Education, French Bull Dog Club of America

This book is a wonderful resource for anyone interested in becoming a judge of the French Bulldog. If you want to become a judge of Frenchies, you should not only study this chapter but also the other chapters, particularly the history of the breed and the chapter on French Bulldog health and anatomy. All of this information will be useful to educate yourself about the breed. Do remember that the French Bulldog has always been a companion animal and has never had a "function" except to be a lap dog, but it's also important to remember the breed's relationship to the Bulldog. Much of what is called for in the French Bulldog standard goes back to the Bulldog standard in which the requirements of the dog—the head, roach/wheel back, etc.—had a functional explanation. These were characteristics that were needed in a dog used for bullbaiting.

The United States is credited with having the first written standard for the French Bulldog. Written in 1898, the standard has been amended only three times since that date. The standard is quite simple and is based in large part upon the Bulldog standard with a few significant differences. However, what we have today has actually changed very little from the original French Bulldog standard. The most recent revision, approved in 1991 at the request of the AKC to meet formatting requirements, introduced a weight disqualification and a description of gait; it also eliminated the point system.

In judging the French Bulldog it is important to remember what the standard calls for in the section on general appearance, particularly its description of the French Bulldog as an "active, intelligent, muscular dog of heavy bone, smooth coat, compactly built and of medium or small structure." The reference to medium or small structure refers back to earlier standards, which specified in the section on weight that there was a lightweight

The French Bulldog

class under 22 pounds and a heavyweight class of 22 pounds but not over 28 pounds. These separate weight classes were eliminated in the 1991 standard, but it does stipulate that no preference is to be made between a French Bulldog with a small structure and one with a medium structure.

The next paragraph of the standard, which defines what is asked for in proportion and symmetry, is also important: "All points are well distributed and bear good relation one to the other; no feature being in such prominence from either excess or lack of quality that the dog appears poorly proportioned."

The standard specifies that the ideal French Bulldog should be a compact (short-bodied) dog with good bone for his size, short legs, roach back and short low-set tail, with a large head with bat ears, and that all of these features are to be in such balance that no one feature stands out. (Interesting to mention, The (British) Kennel Club standard notes that the bat ears and the short undocked tail are the characteristic features of the breed.) The large square head should be in balance with the rest of the body: the head should not be too big and the neck too short in relation to the rest of the body, or so small that the dog appears to be pinheaded. The dog must not be flat-backed, too high on leg, long-backed or fine-boned. The body, when viewed from above, should be pear-shaped like the Bulldog. The standard also reminds us about the influence of sex and states that "due allowance is to be made in favor of bitches which do not bear the characteristics of the breed to the same marked degree as do the dogs." (This wording almost duplicates that of the Bulldog standard.)

Starting out with the information in these paragraphs, let's go over what goes into judging the French Bulldog, using the details in the rest of the standard as our guide. In evaluating a French Bulldog, or any table breed, keep in mind the old saw that "you evaluate the dog on the table and judge him on the floor."

When a class of French Bulldogs enters the ring, whether it is a class of one or a larger class, you have your first opportunity to assess the quality of the dogs. In instructing the Frenchies to go around the ring, you will get a good idea of the overall quality of the dogs, how their outlines conform to what the standard calls for in terms of balance and proportion and how sound the dogs are. The most important time you will spend is in going over the French Bulldogs on the table. This is your opportunity to have your hands on each dog.

After the exhibitor has set the dog up on the table, evaluate the dog first in profile from at least four feet away and then from the front so that you get a good picture of the overall balance and proportion of the dog. In profile the dog's roach back should be obvious. The section in the standard on size, proportion and substance adds to what has already been specified in the aforementioned paragraphs, which are the first two paragraphs of the standard. While the standard says that the dog is supposed to be compact, it doesn't say that the dog should be square, slightly off-square or short-coupled, nor does it include any details on what the ideal height of a male or female French Bulldog should be.

Facing page: The Frenchie should be a compact dog with good bone and muscle. The ideal head is large but not out of proportion with the rest of the body.

After looking at the dog from a distance, it's time to go over him. Start by approaching him from the front. The French Bulldog head is the hallmark of the breed; the former point scale allocated 40 out of 100 total points to the head and its various aspects. The head should be "large and square," with round moderate-sized eyes that are set far apart, bat ears, a flat skull, in proportion a slightly rounded forehead, a well-laid-back muzzle and a well-defined stop with heavy wrinkles over the extremely short nose, which must be black except for light-colored dogs. The French Bulldog should have a deep, square, broad underjaw that is undershot and well turned up.

Examining the head does not require a lot of manual manipulation to see what is correct and what is incorrect. The French Bulldog is a brachycephalic breed and should have an undershot bite. If the bite is correct, you should be able to tell without even opening the dog's mouth to look at his bite. If the dog is overshot or has a wry mouth, that is also quite obvious. You can also tell whether the dog has a nice wide underjaw or whether it is too narrow.

The AKC requires judges to look inside each dog's mouth, so it is important to learn how to examine the bite properly. If you are rough with a dog, you can ruin a show career. The easiest way to look at the dog's bite is to hold the head with both hands and use your thumbs to flip up the flews, "black, thick and broad, hanging over the lower jaw at the sides," and peek into the mouth to see how wide the underjaw is and to see if the top and bottom jaws are correctly aligned. The standard specifies an undershot jaw, but does not specify to what degree. It is preferable that the teeth not show when the mouth is closed, it is preferable that the bite not be wry, and it is preferable that the tongue not show when the mouth is closed, but none of this is mentioned in the standard. There is no reason to check for missing teeth, since the standard does not call for complete dentition and there is no mention of missing teeth being a fault. You may notice that some French Bulldogs have extra incisors but, again, this is not mentioned in the standard. While you are holding the dog's head to examine the bite, take the time to feel the dog's underjaw to make sure it is curved as called for in the standard: "The underjaw is deep, square, broad, undershot and well turned up."

When you are judging the French Bulldog and examining his bite, do not try any of the following techniques: Do not examine the bite by sticking your

The French Bulldog

thumb or thumbnail into the dog's mouth and feeling the teeth. You may cut the dog's gums this way and make him back away from the judge the next time a judge goes to examine the bite. Do not examine the bite by using your hands to lift up the flews from above. If you do, you may partially cover the dog's eyes or nostrils. Flat-faced breeds do not like this. Do not ask the exhibitor to show the dog's bite. This requires the exhibitor to let go of the leash, to use both hands to hold the underjaw and to lift up the flews. Young dogs in particular won't want to stand still for this and may back up or try to jump off the table.

After checking the bite, make sure that the eyes are the correct size, shape, color and placement. When the dog is looking forward, you should not be able to see the whites of the eyes. The eye rims should be black (or dark in cream-colored dogs) and the dog should have adequate fill under the eyes.

The most important feature that differentiates the French Bulldog's head from that of his English cousin are the bat ears. A French Bulldog without bat ears must be disqualified. Make certain that the bat ears are of correct shape, placement and size. The standard does not specify exactly what the size should be, though it does say the following: "Ears, known as the bat ear, broad at the base, elongated, with round top, set high on the head but not too close together, and carried erect with the orifice to the front."

About the nose, the standard notes, "Nostrils black. Nose other than black is a disqualification, except in the case of lighter colored dogs, where a lighter colored nose is acceptable but not desirable." A brindle, a brindle pied or a white Frenchie that does not have a black nose must be disqualified.

Most Frenchies have nostrils that give the appearance of being narrow; this is acceptable as long as the dog appears to have no breathing problems. It's obvious when a dog has trouble breathing: he may appear short of breath or his breathing may be noisy because his nostrils are constricted and his palette is too long. A dog with an elongated soft palate and stenotic nares, conditions that are intimately associated, is very noisy when he breathes and particularly when he moves. The dog may look like a goldfish when he inhales because he can't get adequate air intake through his nostrils, so he breathes through his mouth. This is very undesirable in a dog whose suitability as a breeding animal is being evaluated.

Note the wrinkles as mentioned in the standard. These are the wrinkles located on the muzzle, where "heavy wrinkles form a soft roll over the extremely short nose." Most of the examination of the head is front-on, but be sure to look at the head in profile, checking to make sure that the muzzle layback is correct. The nose is supposed to be very short and the underjaw well turned up. The dog should not look nosey, that is, have a longer, flatter muzzle, which occurs in a dog whose repandus (underjaw) is too flat and doesn't have the desired curvature. The stop should be well defined.

Brindle, brindle and white, white and brindle (i.e., brindle pied) and white French Bulldogs must have a solid black noses. A dog of any of these colors

Facing page: This young Frenchie has no trace of brindle in the black patches, which is a disqualification for the show ring.

that has a butterfly nose or a pink nose should be disqualified. Note that it is very rare to see a white French Bulldog; basically a white French Bulldog is a white and brindle dog with no brindle patches anywhere, so the dog's nose has to be black. Cream-colored French Bulldogs may have the appearance of being white, or almost white, but they usually have some light biscuiting on their ears, and their noses will be lighter in color, not black like a white Frenchie's. Cream is a dilute color; some creams have dark noses, but never jet black. A cream French Bulldog typically has darker eye rims, whereas a white French Bulldog would have pink eye rims. Some fawn Frenchies, particularly the ones without black masks, have lighter-colored noses. Some novice exhibitors of cream French Bulldogs will use enhancements to dye their dogs' noses black. If you determine that the dog's nose color has been altered, if the dye rubs off on a tissue, the dog should be disqualified.

Once you have finished evaluating the dog's head, take a step back and evaluate the front of the dog. The front legs are supposed to be "short, straight, muscular and set wide apart." Looking at the front while the dog is on the table, the space formed by the chest, ground and front legs should form a square. The compact feet, moderate in size with short nails, should face forward. The legs should not be bowed and the feet should toe neither in nor out. The dog should not look leggy or too wide.

The French Bulldog is a short-haired breed that does not require a lengthy body massage to ensure that everything is correct and in proportion. The front legs are supposed to be short, the chest should be broad and deep and the body is variously described as short, well rounded and compact. When the standard was most recently revised, the committee resisted a recommendation that the French Bulldog should have a very short back.

In going over the body of the French Bulldog, it's a good idea to put your hand between the front legs to evaluate the width and depth of the chest, checking to make certain that the elbows are correctly positioned and the front legs have adequate (heavy) bone.

It is very important to carefully examine the topline of the French Bulldog. Run your hand down the back to ensure that the topline/spine is correct. It should not feel level or flat; rather, it should fall slightly behind the withers and level out over the rib cage. At the start of the loin, the vertebrae should change direction and form a roach (gentle arch) over the loin. (The term "roach" comes from the roach fish, whose body outline is supposedly similar in shape to the Bulldog's and French Bulldog's "roach back.") The best way to locate the start of the loin is to use your hands to find the last rib and determine where it attaches to the spine at the location of the last thoracic vertebrae. The loin starts at the first lumbar vertebra, and you should be able to feel a change of direction and the arching over the loin. The highest point of the roach should be the same height as the highest point of the withers. If the spine starts to rise/change direction over the rib cage, that is incorrect and is called a "camel back." If it starts to rise at the beginning of the loin and goes straight up to the tail, that also is incorrect and is called a "sway back" or "swamp back."

The body should be broad at the shoulders and taper at the waist/loin so that it has a pear shape when viewed from the top. The pear-shaped body is one of the characteristic features of the French Bulldog and the Bulldog, but the Frenchie "pear" is not as robust as that of the Bulldog. When you are judging the dog on the table, you can use your hands to go down the

sides of the body to feel whether it has the correct pear shape; when the dog is on the ground, you can get a better view of the pear shape.

The French Bulldog's tail should be short, be set on low and point down. It can be straight or screwed, but not curly like a Pug's. Check the tail to make sure that it has not been docked, as this is a disqualifying alteration. A tail that is set on high, or a gay tail, is not correct.

The rear legs of the French Bulldog are supposed to be longer than the front legs so that they can elevate the loin. The standard specifies "hocks well let down" with moderate rear angulation. The back feet are basically the same as the front feet: compact toes, well split up with short nails and high knuckles, but they may be slightly longer than the front feet. They should not toe out or appear to be cowhocked or bowed.

Unlike the Bulldog standard, the French Bulldog standard does not list the acceptable colors in order of preference. The standard does include a number of colors that are disqualifications. A solid black French Bulldog must be disqualified. This is a dog that has no trace of brindle (fawn hairs) in the coat. The exhibitor should be able to show you where the trace of brindle is; it will save you time if you ask the exhibitor to show you instead of trying to find it for yourself. Please note: a French Bulldog that appears black but does have a trace of brindle somewhere on his body is just as acceptable as the brindle French Bulldog that has more fawn striping.

"Mouse" is the French Bulldog standard's term for what is called blue in some other breeds. It's highly unlikely that there would be a mouse dog being shown. Liver is another disqualification, and a liver French Bulldog would also have a liver nose. Liver French Bulldogs are extremely rare. Black and tan is another disqualification; the predominant color is black with tan markings on the head, legs and body in a pattern similar to the Rottweiler's. Black and white and white with black are also

disqualifications. White with black is a predominantly white dog with black patches and must have a trace of brindle.

Do not confuse a black-masked fawn with a black and tan. A predominantly fawn French Bulldog with black on the muzzle (mask) and black or darker ears is a perfectly acceptable color and should not be penalized.

Finally, if you have any questions about the dog's being over 28 pounds, do not lift the dog up off the table to see how heavy he is. If you think he might weigh out, you must call for the scale. Have the steward call for the superintendent to bring the scale to the ring. The scale must have a weight to calibrate it. If the superintendent doesn't have the weight to calibrate the scale with, you cannot weigh the dog. The superintendent will show you how to use the scale, as not all scales are alike. Once you have familiarized yourself with how the scale works, put the scale on the table and show the exhibitor, with the use of the weight, that it is properly calibrated. When you've done this, most scales will have to be turned off and on again.

The exhibitor is instructed to put the dog on the scale. Ideally the dog should not be touched by the exhibitor when is he on the scale and should sit or stand still long enough so that the judge and exhibitor can see what the dog weighs. If the dog is under 28 pounds, the judge should mark in his book that the dog has been weighed and what the weight was. If the dog is over 28 pounds, the judge should mark in his book that the dog has weighed out and write down the dog's weight.

Any exhibitor that is in the ring with another dog that he feels could be weighed out has the right to ask the judge to call for the scale. If an exhibitor calls for the scale during the judging of Best of Breed on the dog that won Winners Dog or Winners Bitch, and the dog weighs out, the dog must be disqualified and the Reserve Winner should come into the ring and compete for Best of Winners.

Facing page: Viewed from the front, the Frenchie should have a broad, deep, full chest with straight, strong, widely set forelegs.

On Judging the French Bulldog

Wait to check the dog's expression until the dog is on the floor. Some dogs are not all that happy when they are on the table, and they can do amazing things with their ears! A Frenchie may flatten his ears on his backskull or relax them so it looks as if his ears are coming out of the side of his head. On the other hand, young dogs particularly are so happy-go-lucky that if you talk to them on the table, they may become even more wiggly and difficult to examine; thus it's best to be as quick and as businesslike as possible. But if the exhibitor wants to show you the dog's expression when he's on the table, that's fine.

After you have seen what you need on the table, ask the exhibitor to put the dog on the ground and move him in whatever pattern you prefer. Ask the handler to move on a loose lead and not too fast. In the French Bulldog standard the description of gait is: "Correct gait is double tracking with reach and drive; the action is unrestrained, free and vigorous." He is supposed to have a pear-shaped body, wider in the front and narrower in the rear, which means that when the dog moves away from you, his rear legs should move closer together than the front legs do. When the dog is moving toward you, you should be able to see his rear legs moving closer together. The French Bulldog viewed from the side should have the reach and drive that is appropriate for a compact, short-legged dog with a roach back. The dog should maintain the correct topline (roach) as he moves. The tail carriage should not be gay; the tailset should be low and the tail should point down.

When the dog returns to you, evaluate his expression. The exhibitor should be able to show you the dog's expression, with either bait or a toy; if the exhibitor is a novice, you as judge can try and get expression out of the dog when he is on the floor. The French Bulldog is supposed to have an alert, curious and interested expression. The ears should not be set on too high like a donkey's or look as if they coming from the sides of his head. Thinking of the ears as the hands of a clock, they should be placed as if they are set on 11:00 and 1:00. "10 and 2 will not do!"

Temperament in the French Bulldog is very important. Frenchies should be "well behaved, adapt-

able, and comfortable companions with an affectionate nature and even disposition; generally active, alert, and playful, but not unduly boisterous." Dogs that do not have these qualities should be penalized; this would include, but is not limited to, a shy dog that is difficult to examine, a dog-aggressive French Bulldog, a dog that will not walk on the lead or a dog that growls at the judge or at his owner.

After checking the dog's movement going down and back and evaluating his expression, you can check his side movement as he goes around the ring. In classes with multiple dogs, after examining all dogs in the class individually, you may ask the exhibitors to face the dogs front on. This gives you the best opportunity to compare the dogs' fronts. Moving behind the row of dogs set up in this fashion, you can also look over the dogs' bodies from behind to see whether they have the correct pear shape. Ask the exhibitors to set them up again in profile to compare toplines, and then you should be able to make your selections. If you need to reexamine something in one or more of the dogs in a class that you've already gone over, ask the exhibitor to put the dog back on the table and reexamine whatever you want to check again.

When it comes to making a choice for Winners Dog and Winners Bitch, do not be surprised if the best dog comes from the Puppy Class, or is a puppy entered in the Bred-by-Exhibitor Class. French Bulldogs mature early and can finish their championships from the Puppy Class.

In judging Best of Breed, the same procedure should be followed. A dog that is entered in Breed competition should be expected to be better behaved and more polished than some of the younger dogs entered in the Puppy Classes. However, with that in mind, you should not hesitate to put up a class dog over a class of champions. The temperament described in the French Bulldog standard calls for an intelligent, happy, confident dog, and this is a dog that enjoys being shown. If you find what you like in a dog that is not finished, do not hesitate to send this dog to the Group ring.

The French Bulldog is a delightful breed. A well-put-together Frenchie that fits the standard and has the personality to match is a joy to behold. Enjoy your judging of this charming and attractive breed!

AMERICAN KENNEL CLUB BREED STANDARD (REVISION 11-2-90)

General Appearance

The French Bulldog has the appearance of an active, intelligent, muscular dog of heavy bone, smooth coat, compactly built, and of medium or small structure. Expression alert, curious, and interested. Any alteration other than removal of dewclaws is considered mutilation and is a *disqualification*.

Proportion and Symmetry—All points are well distributed and bear good relation one to the other; no feature being in such prominence from either excess or lack of quality that the animal appears poorly proportioned.

Influence of Sex—In comparing specimens of different sex, due allowance is to be made in favor of bitches, which do not bear the characteristics of the breed to the same marked degree as do the dogs.

Size, Proportion, Substance

Weight not to exceed 28 pounds; over 28 pounds is a *disqualification*. *Proportion*—Distance from withers to ground in good relation to distance from withers to onset of tail, so that animal appears compact, well balanced and in good proportion. *Substance*—Muscular, heavy bone.

Head

Head large and square. *Eyes* dark in color, wide apart, set low down in the skull, as far from the ears as possible, round in form, of moderate size, neither sunken nor bulging. In lighter colored dogs, lighter colored eyes are acceptable. No haw and no white of the eye showing when looking forward. *Ears* Known as the bat ear, broad at the base, elongated, with round top, set high on the head but not too close together, and carried erect with the orifice to the front. The leather of the ear fine and soft. Other than bat ears is a *disqualification*.

The top of the *skull* flat between the ears; the forehead is not flat but slightly rounded. The *muzzle* broad, deep and well laid back; the muscles of the cheeks well developed. The stop well defined, causing a hollow groove between the eyes with heavy wrinkles forming a soft roll over the extremely short nose; nostrils broad with a well defined line between them. *Nose* black. Nose other than black is a *disqualification*, except in the case of the lighter colored dogs, where a lighter colored nose is acceptable but not desirable. *Flews* black, thick and broad, hanging over the lower jaw at the sides, meeting the underlip in front and covering the teeth, which are not seen when the mouth is closed. The *underjaw* is deep, square, broad, undershot and well turned up.

Facing page, top: The Frenchie gait in profile.
Facing page, bottom: A mouse-colored Frenchie; also note the light-colored eyes. This blue color is a disqualification in the French Bulldog.

Neck, Topline, Body

The *neck* is thick and well arched with loose skin at the throat. The *back* is a roach back with a slight fall close behind the shoulders; strong and short, broad at the shoulders and narrowing at the loins. The *body* is short and well rounded. The *chest* is broad, deep, and full; well ribbed with the belly tucked up. The *tail* is either straight or screwed (but not curly), short, hung low, thick root and fine tip; carried low in repose.

Forequarters

Forelegs are short, stout, straight, muscular and set wide apart. Dewclaws may be removed. *Feet* are moderate in size, compact and firmly set. Toes compact, well split up, with high knuckles and short stubby nails.

Hindquarters

Hind legs are strong and muscular, longer than the forelegs, so as to elevate the loins above the shoulders. Hocks well let down. *Feet* are moderate in size, compact and firmly set. Toes compact, well split up, with high knuckles and short stubby nails; hind feet slightly longer than forefeet.

Coat

Coat is moderately fine, brilliant, short and smooth. Skin is soft and loose, especially at the head and shoulders, forming wrinkles.

Color

Acceptable colors—All brindle, fawn, white, brindle and white, and any color except those which constitute disqualification. All colors are acceptable with the exception of solid black, mouse, liver, black and tan, black and white, and white with black, which are *disqualifications*. Black means black without a trace of brindle.

Gait

Correct gait is double tracking with reach and drive; the action is unrestrained, free and vigorous.

Temperament

Well behaved, adaptable, and comfortable companions with an affectionate nature and even disposition; generally active, alert, and playful, but not unduly boisterous.

Disqualifications

Any alteration other than removal of dewclaws. Over 28 pounds in weight. Other than bat ears. Nose other than black, except in the case of lighter colored dogs, where a lighter colored nose is acceptable. Solid black, mouse, liver, black and tan, black and white, and white with black. Black means black without a trace of brindle.

Approved June 10, 1991
Effective July 31, 1991

Amanda West on the train with Ch. Bouquet Nouvelle Ami, "Jo-Jo."

12

Presenting

LA CRÈME DE LA CRÈME

In each decade there have been French Bulldogs who have made a difference in the breed, and that difference can be defined in two ways: the dogs who have been the top producers and the dogs who have kept the breed in the public eye during the years when the breed was considered to be rare. The reader must remember that in the more recent decades, where there have been many more shows and air travel has permitted dogs to get to shows more easily, it has been easier to amass a number of show wins than it was in the middle of the 20th century. In addition, with the large number of shows across the country, there are more opportunities to get a dog to a show and thus the opportunity to finish more champions is much greater than it was in the 1950s and 1960s.

Ch. Terrette's Tourbillon D'Gamin CD
Sire of 29 champions, including Ch. Hampton's Chevalier and
Ch. Terrette's Tourbillon Orage, both top producers.

Ch. Terrette's Tourbillon Orage
Sire of 26 champions.

Ch. Hampton's Chevalier
Sire of 30 champions, including Am./Mex. Ch. Jimmy Lee's
Flip, who gained his championship at the age of seven months and sired 14 champions.

Am./Can. Ch. Bouquet Nouvelle Ami
Owned by Mr. and Mrs. Ralph West, bred by Bernard Strauss, whelped 1951. Won 19 all-breed Bests in Show, placed in the Group top ten from 1956 through 1964, had four all-breed top ten placements, had eight consecutive Bests of Breed at Westminster and had five Group placements at Westminster. Owner-handled.

Ch. Ber-Neil's Jeepers Jackie

Owned by Mr. and Mrs. Ralph West, bred by Mrs. Neil C. McAllister, whelped 1957. Won four all-breed Bests in Show and was the national specialty winner four years in a row. Owner-handled.

Ch. Ralanda Ami Francine

Bred and owned by Mr. and Mrs. Ralph West, whelped 1958. Won 55 all-breed Bests in Show and the Ken-L Ration award 1962. Handled by Jerry Rigden.

Mrs. West wrote in *Dog World* magazine, "We are very happy that so many prominent and well-qualified judges have recognized the Frenchie in the Group and Best in Show line-up and hope that other sensational Groups and Best in Show awards our Frenchie has won will stimulate more interest in the breed and revive the popularity they so rightfully deserve."

Ch. Balihai's Quad

Sire of 13 champions, including Ch. Adams King of the Road, sire of 25 champions; and Ch. Taurustrail Fearless, sire of 24 champions.

Ch. Cox's Goodtime Ace In The Hole

Sire of 25 champions, including Ch. Cox's Goodtime Charlie Brown, who to date is the top-producing sire in the breed with 97 champions to his credit.

Ch. Cox's Goodtime Mindy Lou of K 'n D

A top-producing dam with nine champion get, including Ch. Cox's Goodtime Charlie Brown and Ch. Cox's Goodtime Make His Mark.

Ch. Cox's Goodtime Charlie Brown

Sire of 97 champions, including Ch. Jackpot! Ez Come…Ez Go, sire of 26 champions to date; and sire of Ch. Lefox Goodtime Steel Magnolia, winner of 50 Bests in Show. Sire of many all-breed Best in Show Frenchies.

Ch. Cox's Goodtime Make His Mark

Sire of 26 champions, including the Best of Breed dog at the FBDCA centennial show and himself the Best Veteran dog at the show and winner of the Stud Dog Class.

Ch. LeFox Goodtime Steel Magnolia

A Frenchie that many of us remember, sired by Ch. Cox's Goodtime Charlie Brown. Jane Flowers, her handler, has written the following about Maggie, "It seems like yesterday when Colette (Secher) brought Maggie to me at the Wheaton show in January in 1991 to begin her show career with Stan and me. Colette and Sarah Sweatt had established a friendship and a shared love of the breed a few years previous to the birth of

Above: The Wests' biggest winner and a very successful Frenchie from the late 1950s/1960s is Ch. Ralanda Ami Francine.
Facing page: Ch. Cox's Goodtime Ace In The Hole was a prolific sire; among his get is the top-producing French Bulldog sire to date, Ch. Cox's Goodtime Charlie Brown.

Maggie. Little did I realize on that initial meeting how much this little spitfire of a Frenchie bitch would impact my life!

"Maggie's first show with us was in Columbia, Missouri in March, 1991. She was a real wiggleworm on the table for examination, but she moved around the ring like she owned it. She was awarded a major to finish and Best of Breed over specials. She won her first Group First under Norman Patton in May 1991 and won her first Best in Show that August. She always moved around the ring with a haughty attitude. She developed the habit of trying to spar with the terriers in the best in show ring and lifting her leg to mark her place wherever she encountered a male smell. It was George War that nicknamed her the 'stud bitch.'

"Maggie was actively campaigned from 1991 to 1994. During that time she won 270 Bests of Breed, 50 Group Firsts and six all-breed Bests in Show. She was Best of Breed at Westminster three times, the last time at the age of eight. In 1997, the centennial anniversary show of the FBDCA, with an entry of over 300, she won Veteran Bitch Class and Best of Opposite Sex under Anne Rogers Clark.

"In her later years Maggie traveled everywhere with us in our coach and lived in the house when we were at home. She ruled both the coach and the house like a queen and never would tolerate other dogs in her domain, but she was affectionate to everyone she encountered.

"Maggie enjoyed good health for over 12 years. When she turned 12 in December, we marveled at her spunkiness. It was only about two weeks before her passing that she began to show signs of failing health. It seems to be fate that Colette appeared at the Louisville shows to see her and later that day she passed away in her sleep. She waited to say good-bye to her first mother, staying in control to the end."

Ch. C and D's Laboss Mon Buntin
Bred by Charles and Dorothy West and owned by Wade and Sue Buntin, whelped 1996. Sire of 52 champions to date and second-highest producer in the breed. Sire of Ch. Jackpot! I'm The Boss Of JustUs, who is a multiple all-breed Best in Show

winner and number-one Frenchie in 2003 and 2004. Best of Breed at the age of seven months, Best in Show at the age of two and Best Veteran at FBDCA nationals in 2004. Sue said, "We picked him up at ten weeks of age and he has wrapped us around his toenails from then 'til now! He loves to ride in the car and to chase the goats and geese. He was limited to a two-day show weekend, as he thought he had done his thing and it was time to go home. He likes to see how dirty he can get, under cars and in mud puddles. His favorite food is chicken, and deer liver is a close second. He is in good health and doesn't look any older than he did at the age of four." Sue's closing comment, "I don't know how we lived before Frenchies came into our lives!"

Ch. Bandog's Earnin' Respect
Sired by Ch. Cox's Goodtime Pierre of K 'n D, whelped 1989. Sire of 11 champions and winner of 11 all-breed Bests in Show and over 60 Non-Sporting Group Firsts. Best of Breed at the FBDCA national specialty in 1990, 1992 and again in 1996 from the Veteran Class. Number-one Frenchie in 1990, 1991 and 1992. Owned by Luis and Patty Sosa and later by Mrs. Lee T. Meyer.

Ch. Bandog's One In A Million

Whelped 1992. Used at limited stud, he has sired 36 champions. He won three all-breed Bests in Show, over 30 Non-Sporting Group Firsts, Best of Breed at the 1993 FBDCA national specialty and first Award of Merit at the 1994 and 1996 FBDCA national specialties, and was the 1996 FBDCA stud dog winner. The Sosas said, "He was a wonderful dog to live with, always fun and a great house dog. He lives on through his get and contributions to the breed." Two of his granddaughters are national specialty winners. Owned by Luis and Patty Sosa and Dr. Cheryl McNeil.

Above, top: Ch. Bandog's Earnin' Respect, pictured during one of his FBDCA specialty wins.
Above, bottom: Ch. Bandog's One In A Million was an important sire and had a successful show career of his own.
Facing page: Making her mark with a firecracker personality and an impressive show career was Ch. LeFox Goodtime Steel Magnolia, pictured with handler Jane Flowers.

PART V

BAT EARS ABROAD!

French nanny and children with their faithful Frenchie, from a layette catalog of La Samaritaine department store in Paris. Circa 1920. Courtesy Mary Evans Picture Library.

13

France & the UK:
DUAL CITIZENSHIP

FRANCE

By Penny Rankine-Parsons with information provided by
Jean-Pierre Girard and Michael Ghys, translated by Ms. Rankine-Parsons

If one had to choose just one kennel that has had the greatest impact on the French Bulldog during recent times in France, that honor should go to Jean-Pierre and Françoise Girard's de Landouar kennel. From the beginning of the 1980s, when the breed was still scarce in France, until the first half of the 1990s, the breeding from de Landouar had considerable success in the show ring, and the Girards were awarded the title Grand Prix de L'Elevage (top breeder) from 1988 through 1995 based on that success.

Jean-Pierre considers the dogs from his kennels, three bred by himself and one an import from the UK, to have contributed greatly to the breed in general. Uber-Felix de Landouar, a light brindle dog of pure French lines, was born in 1983. At that time, brindle Frenchies in France were very dark, and this dog had the first super brindle coat color for many years. He sired 170 puppies and was a multi-champion. Boris de Landouar was a pied dog of French lines, born in 1986. He had a superb clear pied coat and was the origin of a well-known line of pied dogs. He sired 125 puppies and was also a multi-champion. Eaulympe de Landouar, a pied French bitch born in 1990, was a multi-champion and the mother of 22 puppies and five multi-champions. Crindles Tender Tamblyn, a brindle dog and a UK import, was born in 1992 and sired 139 puppies.

Jean-Pierre and Françoise Girard have since retired from breeding and judging. Jean-Pierre's final judging appointment was the Centenary Open Show of the French Bulldog Club of England in 2002.

The French Bulldog

of this breeding in many pedigrees today. One of Hibou Doudou de Bayali's sons, who inherited his excellent traits and who was very successful in the show ring, was the brindle male Jules Iénas du Domaine des Ormes.

Another great sire is Moustique du Marais Picton, the result of a successful blend of French and Dutch lines owned by Mme. Bourquin. He was sired by the Dutch dog Laurent-Perrier v.d Zuylenstede and bred by Arnold Hendricks. The progeny of Moustique du Marais Picton are appreciated at shows by many judges, and his reputation has become international. He is a brindle dog who fits the breed standard well and who sires all three colors: brindle, pied and fawn. Although a veteran, he is still extremely sound and he is sought after for the qualities he transmits to his offspring as demonstrated by such dogs as Ogustin-Ferdinand de Fambuena Didaho.

As for the pieds who have influenced the breed, one finds that Mme. Machurat's (Renaissance du Phénix kennel) Hugo v. Berkenwoude; Narco Dollar de Scarborough Hill, owned by Mme. Bernard (Bois de St Cyr kennel); and another son of Narco Dollar, Tadj Mahal du Bois de St Cyr, are featured in many of the pedigrees of the good pied specimens today.

One of the greatest changes in the breed in France is undoubtedly the recognition of the fawn coat color in the French Bulldog and the incorporation of the color into the breed standard in 1994. This was a very important event that had a great influence on breeding, as now formerly avoided lines can and are being used. To date, however, only three fawn French Bulldogs have obtained the title of French Champion. They are all males: Max du Petit Clos Coralin in 1998; Ogustin-Ferdinand de Fambuena Didaho in 2002; and Unic-Passion des Amis de Bi in 2006. Brindles and pieds each have their own classification at French shows, but at the present time fawns are shown alongside the brindles. As the fawn color is increasing numerically and in popularity, the CBF has approached

Succeeding de Landouar's success in the show ring is another kennel, du Domaine des Ormes, which also must be recognized for the contribution it has made to the breed. This breeding is based on the lines from de Landouar with the addition of the Italian bloodlines of the brindle dog Oliver della Picadette.

In addition to these kennels, other great dogs have had significant influence on the breed in recent decades. Mme. Waget, current president of the Club du Bouledogue Français (CBF), owned Hibou Doudou de Bayali, a male brindle of French origin. He sired many champions, including Naf-Naf du Vidame d'Urfé, the first fawn pied used at stud in France, and the pied Monsieur Hubert de la Boisardière. One can find traces

Above: Moustique du Marais Picton has earned an international reputation as an important sire.
Facing page, top: Ogustin-Ferdinand de Fambuena Didaho was the second fawn Frenchie to obtain the title of French Champion, doing so in 2002.
Facing page, bottom: Unic-Passion des Amis de Bi is just the third fawn Frenchie to achieve a French championship, doing so in 2006.

the Fédération Cynologique Internationale (FCI) for a separate classification for fawn Frenchies.

A mention must be made of a line in France that was noted for its longevity during this period: that of Mme. Greffrath, whose affix is Moulin du Mas Rougier. She regularly bred dogs that reached almost 15 years of age. They were descended from Franco-English lines, but sadly this breeding no longer exists.

With regard to changes in type, during the 1990s a heavier, more extreme Frenchie was the fashion, but today the tendency is to return to a type with less exaggeration that conforms more closely to the breed standard. It should be noted that the dogs who are currently winning at shows are closely related through their pedigrees to those who were winning a few years ago.

Nowadays in France, le Bouledogue Français has become "a la mode." Everyone wants a Frenchie, but unfortunately this newfound popularity has brought many disadvantages to the breed. The number of puppies born had been perfectly stable during the 1970s and half of the 1980s, around 200 annually. From 1985 to 1990 it was a bit higher, close to 350. After that, the numbers have increased every year, reaching 1,600 in 2000 and almost doubling to 3,168 in 2004.

Unfortunately, quality in the breed has not always followed in the same way. Many new to breeding do not have the experience or knowledge to produce Frenchies of good type and so in France, in the last few years, French Bulldogs of the very best and worst type can be found. However, the Club du Bouledogue Français, dedicated to preserving the health and well-being of the French Bulldog, has risen to the challenge and has taken many steps to encourage novice breeders to learn more about the breed. They publish an excellent quarterly magazine, which contains health articles and general information on the breed, and have a very informative web site. The CBF, working closely with the Société Centrale Canine, will soon offer guidelines for the selection of breeding

pairs, which will include health requirements such as x-rays of the spine, respiratory tests and temperament tests. Genetic identification is highly encouraged to ensure that pedigrees are correct and to prevent misrepresentation. The CBF has produced a Code of Ethics for its members, designed to respect and preserve the welfare of the French Bulldog. The club has also a well-supported rescue network presided over by Mme. Bourquin.

As we well know, the Internet has made it possible to establish contacts worldwide with breeders and enthusiasts who share the same passion. France, like the UK, is choosing to become less isolated from the rest of the world. It is a wonderful opportunity to share our knowledge, experiences and passion for the French Bulldog.

UNITED KINGDOM
By Penny Rankine-Parsons

In the UK from 1985 to the present there have been a number of constant and well-established French Bulldog kennels. Bomlitz, Nokomis, Quatt and Tommyville have continually produced quality Frenchies. Looking at their achievements in the show ring, these kennels have had considerable influence within the breed. There are, of course, more recently established breeders coming to the fore, but those gaining the most success have kennels built on these traditional lines. To name but a few, Lucy Bonsal (Muggshotts), Philip Stemp (Laudernell), Paul Pearce (Hetana) and Penny Rankine-Parsons (Penburton), all of whom are skillfully blending the traditional lines of Bomlitz, Nokomis, Tollydane, etc., are producing sound Frenchies of excellent type, which bodes well for the future of the breed.

The Bomlitz affix is owned by Mrs. Vivien Watkins, president of the French Bulldog Club of England and chairman of the French Bulldog Club of England Welfare Trust (breed rescue). Mrs. Watkins's kennel was established in the 1940s and based on the successful lines of that time. She is the most eminent authority on French Bulldogs in the UK, a skillful and knowledgeable breeder with the greatest empathy for the breed. The breed and its fanciers owe her very much. We are very fortunate to have Bomlitz continuing to exert a strong influence on the breed with some promising offspring from Ch. Shanvic Noir Bear Bomlitz, the latest champion owned by Mrs. Watkins, currently having success in the show ring. Jafrax Bear Skin Under Senkra took the Dog Challenge Certificate (CC) at the Manchester Championship Show 2006, and Penburton Abracadabra won the Dog CC with Best of Breed at the French Bulldog Club of England 2006 Championship Show; these two dogs are "Noir Bear" sons. The trademarks of the Bomlitz Frenchies are their wonderful soft expressions, the darkest of eyes and straight fronts with sound pasterns. Bomlitz champions traditionally have not been campaigned further after achieving their titles.

Maureen Bootle, a talented and successful breeder with many champions to her credit and who is past president of the Midlands and Northern Counties French Bulldog Club (M&NFBC), is owner of the Tommyville Frenchies, which were established during the late 1960s. After her early success she went to live in Sweden for a while and then returned to the UK at the end of the 1980s, bringing with her some of the Tommyville Frenchies. Once more, they soon made their presence felt in the show ring.

One of the most recent French Bulldogs that has influenced her line is the brindle dog Ch. Mid Ship Man of Vardene, joining the Tommyvilles in 2001 almost by chance at the age of 18 months. Winner of 13 CCs, his most spectacular win was Best in Show at the French Bulldog Club of England's Centenary

Facing page, top: Muggshotts Casanova, of Lucy Bonsal's Muggshotts kennel.
Facing page, bottom left: Owned by the UK's French Bulldog authority Vivien Watkins is Eng. Ch. Shanvic Noir Bear Bomlitz (LEFT) and his father, Eng. Ch. Renebeck Renown of Bomlitz.
Facing page, bottom right: Remembered as one of the breed's most prolific sires in the UK is Eng. Ch. Tollydane Pierrot at Nokomis.

Bomlitz Berthier (a son of White Bear) and bred by Messrs. Blagrave and Hutchings, did not go on to produce outstanding offspring. Another outstanding Frenchie was Ch. Snowman Nokomis (Nokomis White Bear ex Byrock Miss Jade), bred by Mrs. J. Mail. This important pied male is behind some of the best clear pieds seen in recent decades.

Probably by far the most influential stud dog since 1985 is Nokomis White Bear's son, the very prolific Ch. Tollydane Pierrot at Nokomis (Nokomis White Bear ex Tollydane le Must de Cartier). He sired 139 puppies born between 1986 and 1994 and was the top stud dog between 1990 and 1995. Many of his unions formed the basis of other French Bulldog kennels.

For the world-famous Bulldog kennel of Mr. Chris Thomas and Mr. Graham Godfrey (Kingrock), the unions of Ch. Tollydane Pierrot at Nokomis with their homebred Frenchie, Kingrock Saffron, produced four UK champions, Eng. Ch. Kingrock Bush Basil, Eng. Ch. Kingrock Peppermint, Eng. Ch. Kingrock Bergamot and Eng./Am. Ch. Kingrock Poppyseed as well other champions overseas. Pierrot also sired champions Jolerob Xplorer and Xtravert, owned by Barry and Betty Wright (Crindle), and Jolerob Second Time Around. These three all went on to produce further winning offspring for Crindle, Jolerob and Vardene, to name but a few.

Ch. Tollydane Pierrot at Nokomis was also the sire of Firedancer at Glenlee, a top stud dog bred by Mr. Stevenson and owned by the Drummonds. Firedancer formed the basis of the Glenlee kennels, which are best known for their fawn Frenchies. Two or three of their fawn males have been exported in recent years and have had a good influence on the breed, particularly in the Eastern European countries.

The Quatt kennel was established in the early 1950s, and Quatt Frenchies can be found in the pedigrees of French Bulldogs worldwide. From 1985 onward, there were five Quatt Frenchies who gained their championships in the UK, the last being Quatt

Show under Mrs. Vivien Watkins. "Moley," as he is known, is the sire of many winning offspring, the most famous being Ch. Birique Prinzessin, a beautiful black-masked clear fawn bitch bred by Neil Birks of Birique French Bulldogs.

Jill Keates, another formidable breeder of champions and a vice president of the M&NFBC, is the owner of the famous Nokomis lines, which were established just a little later than Tommyville. Needless to say, Nokomis pedigrees were built on the successes of previously established lines.

Credit must be given to Nokomis White Bear who, though he never gained his title, sired a number of outstanding champions including the famous brindle bitch Ch. Nokomis Omeme, the breed record-holder for many years. Unfortunately, Ch. Nokomis Omeme and the current breed record-holder, Ch. Merrowlea The Enchantress, sired by

Above: Eng./Am. Ch. Kingrock Poppyseed was but one of the champions sired by Eng. Ch. Tollydane Pierrot at Nokomis
Facing page: Laudernell Keltic Prince of Philip Stemp's Laudernell kennel.

Paddington of Ferryland, owned by the late Judith Sidney. With the sudden and unexpected death of Ann Cottrell in April 2001, the Quatt kennel ceased to exist. Sadly, and despite all efforts from the French Bulldog Club of England Welfare Trust, the Quatt Frenchies were dispersed and the lines have been lost to the serious breeder.

Tollydane kennels have also disappeared. Their successful lines were based on established lineage from Quatt and Bomlitz. This kennel imported Rajah v.d. Grimmelsburg from Germany and incorporated his bloodlines into the traditional English breeding. The very sound pied dog Hetana Ringmaster (a double grandson of Ch. Rajah v.d. Grimmelsburg), owned and bred by Paul Pearce, is producing some very typey and winning offspring, although he is not shown.

The owners of the Wilcott French Bulldogs, whose lines were Tommyville based, have retired and are no longer breeding Frenchies. Their lines live on, however, as they form the foundation stock for Rosgave, another young kennel.

Annual litter registrations with The Kennel Club remain fairly constant, with between 250 and 350 pups born per year in recent years. Breeders in the UK are lucky that The Kennel Club will allow them to endorse the pedigrees of their puppies with "Progeny not eligible for registration," and the majority of reputable breeders will do so. Breeders are also able to add another endorsement: "Not eligible for the issue of an export pedigree." Both of these clauses, along with the breeders' standard contracts of sale, have helped to keep our pups out of the hands of the less scrupulous breeders, but unfortunately there are still a few. The demand for the French Bulldog still outweighs the supply, so reputable breeders are always able to find good homes for their puppies.

Frenchies from the UK are rarely exported, with an average of 13 dogs per year being sent abroad. Imports, too, are infrequent, with only 17 Frenchies coming into the UK between 1985 and 2005, nine of those being pets. Even with the relaxation of the UK's quarantine regulations, imports have not increased.

In recent decades in the UK there have been, on average, between three and six French Bulldogs gaining their championship status each year. The UK still remains the most difficult country in which to earn a championship in any breed. Because of this, many worthy French Bulldogs go unnoticed by the general fancy, as they do not sport titles.

The French Bulldog Club of England Welfare Trust (the club's rescue scheme) probably deals with about six to ten rescue cases a year, mostly Frenchies needing new homes due to changes in their owners' circumstances. Thankfully it is extremely rare for them to have to deal with a cruelty case.

Taken as a whole, the breed is in fine fettle in the UK. Type can vary, but as linebreeding is the norm, established breeders continue to produce Frenchies that come close to the breed standard. Size continues to be a concern, as well as rear movement. With health issues in mind, the following amendments to the French Bulldog breed standard were approved by The Kennel Club and became effective on January 1, 2006:

General Appearance: Sturdy, compact solid small dog with good bone, short, smooth coat. No point exaggerated, balance essential. Dogs showing respiratory distress highly undesirable.

Gait/Movement: Free and flowing. Soundness of movement of the utmost importance.

Above: Penburton Abracadabra, owned by Penny Rankine-Parsons, took the Reserve CC at Crufts 2007.
Facing page, top left: Ch. Mid Ship Man of Vardene, who won Best in Show at the French Bulldog Club of England's Centenary Show.
Facing page, top right: The influence of Eng. Ch. Snowman Nokomis is felt today in some of the breed's outstanding pieds.
Facing page, bottom: Max du Petit Clos Coralin was the first and is one of the few fawn French Bulldogs to obtain the title of French Champion, doing so in 1998.

Coming to Australia in 1995, Aus. Ch. Guy Laroche de la Parure was the first French Bulldog imported to the country from the Netherlands.

14

The Road to
OZ
& New Zealand

By Michael Rosser

How and when did the French Bulldog establish itself in Australia and New Zealand as a recognized breed? Permit some detective work—a process of elimination, if you will—as well as some global backtracking.

We know that the years 1896 to 1905 saw the French Bulldog come to prominence. The breed, with its bat ears, was championed in America, became well recognized in France (though with ear arguments), was resisted and eventually accepted in England and was generally welcomed or already established in Germany, Austria, Belgium and Switzerland. The breed's establishment in Holland came a couple of years later, in 1907.

In 1897 notables of the Russian Court were seen (of course pre-revolution) in the south of France, where "the bat-eared toy dog is a common sight, and the Russians will have no other." This is a quote from a press interview of George N. Phelps of Boston, who brought Frenchies Monsieur Babot and Ninette from Paris to America in 1896 and successfully showed them that same year. Phelps went on to state: "The Count de Bylandt, of Brussels, who has just published one of the most exhaustive and authoritative books on dogs ever written, specifically states that all toy or dwarf bulldogs should have bat ears, and all illustrations show these ears." That work was described as the most solid cynological publication ever issued, the most comprehensive of the period and "a brilliant Panorama" with the choicest engravings.

What of the dog world in 1897 on the other side of the world from America and Europe? Thanks to one Walter Beilby, we have a great deal of information about the dog world in Australia and New Zealand at the time.

The Dog in Australasia (George Robertson, 1897) was stated by Beilby to be "the first of the kind ever published in the Australasian colonies." The book has been described in our times as a "very solid work of great importance…the first major cynological publication in Australasia…the only reliable guide to the history of British importations arriving and developing there since 1880."

The first dog show in Australia was on April 7 and 8, 1864 (only five years after England's first dog show on June 28 and 29, 1859 at Newcastle). At that first show held in Melbourne, Victoria, 17 entries were recorded in the class for Bulldogs, according to the catalog.

Dogs were imported into Australia and New Zealand only from England. They came by a 40-day steamer or a 140-day ship and had to spend six months in quarantine because of fear of rabies. Walter Beilby studied the quarantine records, which provided him with a valuable source of information about the various breeds coming to Australia. Despite great detail about the Bulldog (including a large folding pedigree table), it seems that no Toy Bulldogs or French Bulldogs had reached the Antipodes by 1897 (or indeed by ten years later).

Was this due to fear of climatic conditions in Australia and New Zealand? Henry St. John Cooper, in his *Bulldogs and Bulldog Men* (1908), stated the following in his section headed "Bulldogs in Australia": "The average man has probably formed the opinion that successful breeding and rearing of Bulldogs in a hot climate is practically an impossibility. Such, however, is by no means the experience of this lady, who is one of the most enthusiastic and successful of Bulldog owners in the land of the Southern Cross."

The lady in question was May Thomson of Richmond, Victoria, Australia. St. John Cooper wrote, "Mrs. Thomson's experiences are of such general interest, especially to those dwelling in tropical climates, that no excuse is necessary for giving them space here…Mrs. Thomson writes as follows, 'I have no trouble with my dogs: Bulldogs thrive and look well, in fact better than ordinary dogs, even under the trying circumstances of the terrible heat of this country. The day on which the last dog I imported arrived, it was 115 degrees in the

shade, but I can assure you in countries such as this, where the grass is all shrivelled up by the sun, my dogs made up for it by eating grapes, green figs, bananas and green fig-leaves (which) very satisfactorily take the place of the grass they would naturally require. This stuff is very similar to spinach. I give them food in plenty, as much as they want, and in the cool of the night I let them have as much meat as they can eat with vegetables that grow above the ground. Meat here is extremely cheap and of splendid quality all the year round. I have never had a case of distemper, and I attribute my use of fruit in the complete banishment of it from my kennels, and I confidently recommend grapes and figs to all who live in tropical climates where fruit grows practically wild. My kennels stand under the shade of grape-vines and peach trees, of which my dogs eat their fill, and it would be impossible to find dogs even in temperate climates as strong and hardy and so entirely free from disease as mine are."

When did the French Bulldog first appear in Australia or New Zealand? Here is what we have: "A friend of my mother told me, when I had my first one, that her grandmother had a Frenchie, I think that must have been before the First World War [1914–1918]—Have also heard of one or two in the '20s—but only pets." Kath Parlett (Sans Tache) of Black Rock, Victoria wrote this in an August 15, 1995 letter to your scribe's wife, Liz Davidson.

What was involved in bringing a French Bulldog from England to Australia or New Zealand in the late 1920s and early 1930s? The export information stated the following:

"To Fremantle, Adelaide, Melbourne and Sydney, if dimensions of kennel supplied by shippers do not exceed 5 feet in length and 3 feet in width, 7 guineas each dog. Over 5 feet in length but not exceeding 9 feet, and over 3 feet wide and not exceeding 4 feet 6 inches, 14 guineas each dog. Over these dimensions to be arranged.

"Dogs are only accepted in cargo steamers; a kennel must be provided, and sufficient food for the voyage. They are placed in charge of an attendant selected from

Facing page: Aus. Ch. Strawbyn Solo was a 1972 import from the UK. He was the sire of the first Frenchie to win Best in Show at an Australian all-breeds championship show.

the crew by the Commander, and a suitable gratuity, to be arranged, is collected with the freight, and the Agency at the port to which the dog is shipped is instructed to pay him the amount arranged on out-turn. (Peninsular and Oriental Steam Navigation Company, 122, Leadenhall Street, E.C.3.) London to Melbourne, Sydney, Newcastle, Brisbane, Auckland, Wellington, Lyttleton, Dundein, the charge is £7:7s., the owner of the dog supplying kennel and food. A veterinary certificate is required. (The Commonwealth and Dominion Line, Ltd., 9, Fenchurch Street, E.C.3.)"

On another route there is this stern admonition: "The owner is expected to give the butcher a small gratuity." Further instructions included: "Owners supplying food for their animals should make allowances for at least two days' emergency rations. Dogs must be placed in the charge of the butcher, and are not allowed in cabins, saloons or on the bridge deck. Animals born on the voyage must be paid for at the appropriate rate.

Special 'all in' rates can be obtained where it is desired that the steamer should provide food and/or kennels."

The dog paper *Dog World* in Australasia stated on April 17, 1935, "It is not almost impossible to get a dog here from America. It is impossible. Dogs are not allowed into Australasia from any part of the world except Britain. Rabies is unknown in Australasia." Even as late as 1937 the same dog paper expressed the opinion that "The Commonwealth Government showed a considerable amount of wisdom when they framed an enactment that no dog could be landed in Australia unless from Britain, now free of rabies."

The first record of a French Bulldog Down Under was when an imported Frenchie was whelped in New Zealand in 1933. These were the bureaucratic conditions imposed in the early 1930s: "THE FOLLOWING CONDITIONS HAVE TO BE COMPLIED WITH IN THE CASE OF DOGS SHIPPED FROM THE UNITED KINGDOM TO NEW ZEALAND. The animal must have been in the United Kingdom from birth, or for nine months preceding shipment. The owner of the dog must fill up a special Declaration Form and sign it before a

Justice of the Peace or Commissioner of Oaths within fourteen days preceding shipment. The dog has to be examined by a local veterinary surgeon, and the certificate at the bottom of the form referred to completed by him. Prior to being put on board ship, the dog has to be further examined by the veterinary surgeon duly appointed by the New Zealand Government, to whom the abovementioned Declaration Form must be handed. Shipments may only take place at London, Liverpool or Glasgow, and on arrival in New Zealand dogs are quarantined at Auckland, Wellington or Lyttelton for a period of two months, at a cost of 4d. per night per dog."

Barkston Dent de Lion, a future champion, was owned by Mrs. John Martin of New Zealand and had been bred by Mrs. Townsend Green, by Lady Kathleen Pilkington's Ch. Chevet Tinker ex Barkston Beauvette. This was an illustrious and extraordinary start, as Mrs. Townsend Green was one of the most respected Frenchie authorities in the UK. She was one of the nine founding members of the French Bulldog Club of England (FBCE). Her Roquet 96 (by Boule ex Boulette) won the first French Bulldog show in England, held on April 7, 1903 at Tattersall's in London. Mrs. Townsend Green's renowned Barkston kennel was founded in 1897, had great influence on Frenchie breeding in England in the 1920s and '30s

and continued until 1940. The good lady was president of the FBCE from 1926 to 1944 and died in 1951. New Zealand French Bulldog breeding could hardly have had a better-credentialed start.

One of Dent de Lion's daughters, Julie de Lisle, was whelped in New Zealand in 1935. She was owned by Mrs. Maxwell Walker of de Lisle kennels of Auckland. Campaigned in Australia, she was Best of Breed at the 1938 Sydney Royal Centenary Show and also became a Victorian champion. She subsequently returned to New Zealand, much to Australia's loss.

The other remarkable import to New Zealand in the 1930s was Helen Colman's Zev of Nork. The Nork prefix went back to the first decade of the 20th century. It was one of the leading English prefixes in the 1920s, and Mrs. Colman had a considerable kennel of over 40 Frenchies (those were the days of kennelmaids and kennelmen). Mrs. Colman died in 1929. Her son, Nigel C. Colman (a member of Parliament), carried on the prefix for some years, but it is possible that the dog came to New Zealand as a consequence of Mrs. Colman's death. Zev of Nork was also owned by Mrs. Maxwell Walker (de Lisle). He was also shown at the 1938 Sydney Royal and won the Dog Challenge Certificate. He also returned to New Zealand, like Julie de Lisle.

For New Zealand, Australia and England, World War II was from 1939 to 1945. It had a profound effect, even on French Bulldogs and their breeding and survival. In England, from 1939 until the spring of 1945, the FBCE ceased activities and many well-known kennels closed down. Others struggled to exist. In New Zealand the result seems to have been the loss of progeny and lines from the Barkston and Nork imports. In Australia it was not until well after the end of the war that there was a record of the first French Bulldogs imported permanently into that country or registered there.

The year 1949 saw the first French Bulldog litter (one dog and two bitches) registered in Australia, born on October 11, 1949 out of Radclive Henry and Bonham's Close Tourmaline (Jean I. Cochrane's Bonham's Close kennel was one of the major kennels in England in the 1920s and 1930s). Radclive Henry and the bitch Bonham's Close Tourmaline were brindles, with pied backgrounds. They were exported from England to Victoria, Australia by one Group Captain Foden. He obviously had not only sufficient style to import Frenchies but also a sense of humor to have chosen the name Bourbon kennels.

The French Bulldog in Australia saw important publicity in 1948. Yvonne Henderson and her husband A.T. Henderson visited New Zealand from England and then stayed in Australia for four months. With her imported bitch, Morebees Bunny, she won the Group at the Melbourne Royal show under English judge Theo Marples. This was a particularly big win. At that time there was no Group 6 (Utility) or Group 7 (Non-Sporting) in Australia (as there are now). Group 5, which is now Working Dogs, at that time contained all breeds other than Toys, Terriers, Gundogs and Hounds. Morebees Bunny became the first French Bulldog in Australia and New Zealand to win a Best in Group at a major show, and there was substantial press coverage. One report of an interview after a later show is worth quoting in part—a glimpse of the Australian dog scene and the rarity of Frenchies in 1948:

"The Hendersons came out to Australia, to settle, but have since found that they have to go back to England for business reasons, and don't really know when they will come back. On the strength of their original intention they brought their dogs with them. Actually it is Mrs. Henderson who is the dog breeder of the family. She specialises in French bulldogs, and she had the only dog she has left in the dog show yesterday. This was the first time that a French bulldog, one of the rarer species of animals, has been seen at a Ballarat show. The Hendersons also had with them a Pyrenean Mountain dog, another rare species in Australia, but this was only Mrs. Henderson's pet. This dog was also shown. Both the dogs shown won at the Royal Melbourne show recently.

"According to the Hendersons, dog shows in Australia cannot yet compare in size or standard with English shows. Mrs. Henderson pointed out that dog shows in England were a thing apart, and that at the last Cheltenham show there were more than 9,000 entries. Mrs. Henderson is of the opinion that dog showing in Australia is still only in its infancy, but given prominence and developed it will quickly come up to overseas standards. What impressed both Mr. and Mrs. Henderson was the way Australian dog exhibitors overcome difficulties of showing. In England dogs are permitted on trains, trams, buses and taxis, and even in hotels, where exhibitors take their dogs to keep them under observation and care until the showing ..."

Ashmill Prince and Pipistrelle Penelope were imported in 1948 to New South Wales by Mr. A Byrnes. Both Frenchies were sold to wealthy retailer Sam Hordern, who owned Anthony Horderns, at the time the local equivalent of Macy's. The dogs were shown at the 1949 Sydney Royal under English judge Leo Wilson. Ashmill Prince won the prize for Best Non-Sporting exhibit. This was more publicity for a breed unknown to most Australians.

There were no registered litters from this pair, Ashmill Prince and Pipistrelle Penelope. This was particularly unfortunate as Ashmill Prince's sire, Olveston Goblin, was the first post-war English champion and his brother, Bonham's Close Ashmill Emperor, won the Challenge Certificate at Crufts and Best of Breed in 1950.

The year 1950 provided a most useful historical record on the Frenchie in New Zealand. New Zealand had been without its own textbook on dogs. Breeders and exhibitors had to rely on imported books. In 1950 S.H. Rastall self-published *Show Dogs of New Zealand*, "the first book of its kind to be published in the Dominion." It contained "the Standards of the fifty different breeds catered for at New Zealand Shows," fortunately including French Bulldogs.

Mr. Rastall was an all-breed judge, had been secretary of the New Zealand Kennel Club from 1928 to 1942, was regarded as an eminent authority and was owner of the British Bulldog Ch. Suncrest Peacemaker. In his section of the book on French Bulldogs he recorded, "The following are among some of the good ones that have appeared in the show-ring and many of our best ones now being exhibited contain some of the undermentioned in their pedigrees: Barkston Dent de Lion (imp), Madame Beaucaire, Charmaine of Sedgemoor, Leconte de Lisle, Barkston Beauvette, Princess Carrisima, Bonham's Close Tourmaline (imp), Caesar de Lisle, Maurice Chevalier, Beau Brummel of Sedgemoor, Gaspard de Lisle, Le Fils de Pierre,

Grenoville of Sedgemoor, Pierre de Messines."

Which dogs have made an impact on the breed in Australia? Trying to be as objective as possible, let's take a look at some of them.

Aus. Ch. Strawbyn Solo (Strawbyn Spright ex Strawbyn Salote) was imported from the UK and arrived in Australia in 1972. He was bred by Mrs. Wybrants Pearce and owned by Kath Parlett. He was an important sire; among his offspring are English, New Zealand and Australian champions as well as the first French Bulldog to win Best in Show at an all-breed championship show in Australia.

Aus. Ch. Quatt Blanco of Kama (Quatt Snow Dollar ex Eng. Ch. Jayne of Quatt) also was an import from the UK, arriving in Australia in 1977. Bred by Joan Cottrell and owned by Les and Dulcie Partridge, he was the sire of many champions.

BISS/BIS Aus. Ch. Sovereign of Selholme (Eng. Ch. Selholme Dominique ex Topsham Summer Wine) arrived in Australia from the UK in 1980. He was bred by Mr. and Mrs. G. Hooten and owned by Dulcie Partridge and Judith and Alan Miller, and was an outstanding sire. His only litter in the UK produced Eng. Ch. Nokomis Miniwatu, who in turn was the dam of Eng. Ch. Nokomis Omeme, the UK breed record-holder for many years. To quote the late Teddy Mileham (Quais and D'Accord French Bulldogs), "When Sovereign first appeared on the show scene in Australia, exhibitors and anyone connected with Frenchies just 'goggled.' We had certainly never seen anything like him, full of self-assurance, an infectious spirit for fun and naughtiness, he projected that elusive "clown-like" temperament. His substance was greater than any Frenchie we had seen and he oozed quality." Sovereign produced a generation of high-quality show and breeding stock and was a huge asset to the breed in Australia.

BISS Aus. Ch. Tenafly Hot Biscuit (Tollydane in Collusion with Merrowlea ex Eng. Ch. Pollyanna of Merrowlea of Tenafly) came to Australia from the UK in 1985. He was bred by Charles Satchell and owned by Judith and Alan Miller. He won 6 Bests in Show with 8 Challenge Certificates at French Bulldog Club of New South Wales specialty shows. He was the sire of champions, including BISS Aus. Gr. Ch. Topette

The French Bulldog

Big Mac, the first Grand Champion French Bulldog in Australia.

Aus. Ch. Apocodeodar His Lordship of Tenafly (Eng. Ch. Ledormy Square Finch ex Eng. Ch. Apocodeodar Imogen) was an import from the UK who came to Australia in 1985. Bred by Bill and Sylvia Stevenson and owned by Stan and Teddy Mileham, "William" absolutely loathed showing and, despite his excellent breed type, was sparingly shown. However, his progeny, particularly those from the Sovereign line, excelled in the show ring. William sired five specialty Best in Show champions, including the remarkable dogs multi-BISS Aus. Ch. Quais Milord Humphrey and BISS Aus. Ch. Kurrallwyn Fifi.

Aus. Ch. Nokomis White Deer (Bomlitz Shah-rastani ex Nokomis Running Moon) was imported from the UK in 1990. He was bred by Jill Keates and owned by Pat Power. He produced some excellent progeny, 13 champions in all, including BISS Aus. Ch. Mjosa Syldaz Chloe.

Tenafly D'Accord Pearl Drop and Aus. Ch. Jolerob Venturer were imports from the UK owned by Stan and Teddy Mileham and Liz Davidson and Michael Rosser. These two great characters arrived in Australia in 1991. Pearl Drop, a descendant of the Selholme line, produced nine champions from three litters, some of whom went to New Zealand, the US and Europe. Jolerob Venturer also brought much-needed fresh blood to Australia. Venturer sired some excellent progeny in Australia and New Zealand, a total of 20 champions. These two imports were a great asset and building block for the breed in Australia.

Aus./NZ Ch. Kenue Playboy from Tenafly (Wilcott Klown Prince at Enchantya ex Tenafly Oyster Catcher) was bred by Paul Pearce and owned by Stan and Teddy Mileham, Liz Davidson and Michael Rosser. A UK import, he arrived in Australia in 1994. He had a very successful show career, being dual-titled in Australia and New Zealand, and sired champions in Australia and New Zealand, including multi-BISS Aus. Ch. D'Accord D'Amour.

Aus. Ch. Guy Laroche de la Parure (Leopard von Eppies Bargie ex Winny de la Parure) was imported from the Netherlands in 1995 and owned by Carlene Naughton. With the relaxation of Australian quarantine restrictions in the mid-1990s, it became possible to import dogs more easily from Europe and the United States. Guy-Laroche was the first French Bulldog imported from Holland and was a huge boost to the gene pool in Australia. Guy-Laroche produced some quality offspring and helped to improve overall breed type in Australia despite limited breeding.

BISS Aus. Ch. Shi-Fra-Sa's The Viking Hanahaus (Int. Ch. Jacquella Jacquard ex BISS Aus. Ch. Shi-Fra-Sa's Jeanne D'Arc) was imported from Norway in 1997. He was bred by Rigmor Haugen Markeng and owned and imported by Carlene Naughton; after her death, he was owned by Liz Davidson and Michael Rosser. To quote English breed specialist judge Jill

Above: "William," Aus. Ch. Apocodeodar His Lordship of Tenafly, a dog who was sparingly shown due to his dislike for the show ring but who passed his outstanding breed type to his offspring.
Facing page, top: Tenafly D'Accord Pearl Drop and Aus. Ch. Jolerob Venturer both carried strong bloodlines, producing champions in multiple countries and bringing fresh blood to the breed in Australia.
Facing page, bottom: BISS Aus. Ch. Shi-Fra-Sa's The Viking Hanahaus is a Norwegian import who has had a profound impact on both Australian and New Zealand breeding programs.

quarantine regulations and all that they involve. Despite all of this, and more, breeders in both countries continue to import French Bulldogs. The desire to breed quality dogs really does override the problems.

Since 2000 the gene pool has increased substantially with imported dogs and bitches from England, Holland, Norway, Switzerland, the United States and Canada. Considering the relatively small number of puppies registered each year, when you compare it with the registration statistics in other countries, it is obvious that breeders are striving to improve the breed without thought (or likelihood) of financial reward. Australian National Kennel Council registrations were around 50 per year in the mid- to late 1980s, and now annual registrations hover around the 250 mark.

With increasing awareness of health issues, strong breed clubs, success in the show ring, doting pet owners and overall interest in the breed, French Bulldogs are in good hands. It is indeed an exciting time Down Under!

Keates of Nokomis French Bulldogs, "Sire of many of my winners today. What an impact this dog has had on the breed…" The Viking has sired over 30 champions in Australia and New Zealand, including 5 specialty Best in Show Winners. He is behind many of the top-winning dogs and kennels in Australia and New Zealand today. His contribution to the breed cannot be overstated.

Breeding and showing dogs in Australia and New Zealand is more of a hobby, a passion if you like, when compared with other countries, such as the United States. Breeders and handlers cannot make a living by showing dogs. Being sports-loving nations with a strong desire to succeed at all levels, Australia and New Zealand possess a determination and will to win that is also very much a part of their dog breeders' psyche.

The difficulties and expenses of importing Frenchies into Australia and New Zealand include having to ship our flat-faced friends on long-distance flights, the dangers of stopovers in the tropics and

PART VI
THE PRICELESS FRENCHIE: ART & *OBJETS D'ART*

A pair of exquisite smoky quartz French Bulldogs decorated with gold and precious gemstones by Russian jeweler Carl Fabergé (1846–1920).

15

Pieces *de* RÉSISTANCE

By Gary Bachman

The unique relationship between people and dogs goes back centuries, and collecting dog-related objects reflects this special bond. In the 19th century it was primarily kennel owners, working to standardize today's breeds, who started to form collections. By the early 20th century many people bred and showed dogs purely as a hobby. At this time they also became aware of the great pleasure of forming collections of dog antiques and collectibles.

The French Bulldog is perhaps the most celebrated dog in art. This is due to the fact that the Frenchie enjoyed the height of its popularity during three important art movements: Victorian, Art Nouveau and Art Deco. The Victorian depictions tend to be highly ornamented while the Art Nouveau models are elegant and sinuous. The Art Deco movement of the 1930s was a response to the Industrial Revolution and gives us pieces that are stylized and decorated in brilliant colors.

The Frenchie's undeniable appeal needs no introduction. Frenchies are, as one breeder stated, "philosophers in the guise of clowns." Another take on this comes from photographer and breeder Colette Séror-Secher, who said, "They think they are little people in dog suits."

Porcelains are by far the most sought after of all Frenchie collectibles. The Germans, in particular, excelled. These pieces range from the sublime to the hilarious. The Danish porcelains reflect a unique sensibility, depicting Frenchies that often have a serious and melancholic demeanor. There are four Austrian factories worth mentioning: Keramos, Augarten, Goldscheider and the Wiener Werkstätte. Both Keramos and Augarten produced a few very fine models. Goldscheider manufactured some of its finest work between 1926 and 1938. It had been rumored that this Jewish-owned factory was destroyed by the Nazis during Kristallnacht, or the "Night of Broken Glass." It was in fact not decimated but taken over by the Nazis in 1938. The owners fled to the United States and opened a factory in New Jersey. The Wiener Werkstätte, or Vienna Workshop (1903–1932), was a Secessionist art movement dedicated to a new concept of design. Its aim was to leave behind the classical art of the past and produce art objects and functional items that were original and affordable. There are also some rare pieces from the former Czechoslovakia and other European countries, and the Japanese copied many of the German models while mass-producing some very original ones.

Other media abound and we find the French Bulldog depicted in bronze and other metals, paintings, drawings, posters, wood, jewelry and glass. Most are purely decorative but we also see quite a number of functional items such as lamps, postcards, books, bookends, toys, walking sticks, desktop accessories and clocks. The Frenchie is also frequently seen in the collecting categories of automobilia and tobacciana.

Most of the early pieces are very high quality and expensive because at the start of the 20th century the Frenchie was very much a wealthy person's dog. Famous owners such as French author Colette, King Edward VII, Elizabeth Arden, Ingrid Bergman, J. P. Morgan and Anna Sacher helped further bolster the Frenchie's popularity. Sacher, in particular, was most influential in popularizing the breed in Vienna. Her brood of French Bulldogs were from the Dernier Cri kennel, which was renowned for many champions. In addition to her celebrated hotel and restaurant, plus the chocolate cake that bears her name, her Frenchies were commemorated on postcards, various gifts to clients and other mementos. Also, the Romanoff Princess Tatiana and Prince Felix Yusupovsky, who allegedly shot Rasputin, owned Frenchies. Appointed court jeweler to the Russian royal family, Carl Fabergé is well-remembered for his

Imperial Easter eggs. He also produced a number of smoky quartz French Bulldogs decorated with gold and precious gemstones. Only a handful of these treasures are known to exist.

Many representations of the French Bulldog are naturalistic, and the dog often sports what is known as a "badger" collar. This classic collar has a standard construction of a leather circlet with real badger hair sticking out on both sides. Not functional, but cosmetic, it aesthetically frames the big Frenchie head and appears as a "halo" around the neck.

We also see the French Bulldog depicted as what has been called a "humanized" dog. Features are caricatured and the most common representation is that of a "bat-eared" clown wearing a double-ruffed circus collar. The Frenchie is sometimes dressed in human clothing; other examples include Frenchies playing tennis, the piano and the drums.

There are two rarefied areas of collecting worth mentioning. First are the lamps. While some are simply bedroom lamps, others are known in German as rauchverzehrer, or "smoke-eaters." These were very popular during the first three decades of the 20th century and are highly sought out by Frenchie collectors today. Made of porcelain with glass eyes and fitted with an electrical socket and bulb, they contain a reservoir into which perfumed oil is poured. When lit, they come alive, while the heat of the light bulb releases a scent to perfume the air in smoke-filled rooms. Only about 25 French Bulldog models are known to exist compared with the myriad of other animal lamps.

Second are the car mascots. Early in the 20th century automobile radiators were large and elegant. Manufacturers adorned the caps with figures or symbols that were unique to each maker, such as the well-known Jaguar mascot. By the 1920s various companies marketed mascots to the well-to-do. Many were designed by some of the best sculptors of the time; the variety is astonishing. Since the Frenchie was so popular during this period, we find a number

Facing page: One of the most superb Frenchies in porcelain, this model with remarkable ears is a great rarity by Metzler & Ortloff with a mark from about 1920.

of fine models though most are now quite rare. Few realize that some of the most superb French Bulldog bronzes are hood ornaments.

Most collectors are familiar with such pieces as the famous Rosenthal whelp or the seated Dahl Jensen Frenchie. While many will recognize a number of the collectibles in this chapter, my aim is to illustrate the rare, unusual and uncommon Frenchie.

Thanks to Françoise and Jean-Pierre Girard, Jan and Jim Grebe, Brenda and Mike Buckles, Alicja Pradella, Manfred Wild, www.muederjoe.com, Stuart King, Bonnie Miller, Hermann-Historica Auctions, Arnold Kieteubl, Camille Stillitano and several private collectors for lending images for this chapter. Special thanks to photographers Lazaro Montano and Terry Lansburgh for many of the fine pictures that follow.

The French Bulldog

Jewelry, Enamel and Gemstones

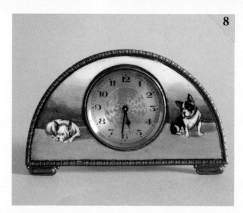

1. A 1903 portrait of Russian Prince Felix Yusupovsky and his fawn Frenchie hangs in the Moscow Museum. After a failed attempt at poisoning Rasputin, the prince allegedly shot him with his revolver. **2.** A fine Austrian silver-enameled pendant from about 1920. **3.** A rare image of the Romanoff Princess Tatiana, with her brindle Frenchie Ortino, and Anastasia. As a pampered Imperial pet, Ortino had collars that were custom-made and set with semiprecious stones by court jeweler Carl Fabergé. **4.** A vintage silver pin of a pair of Frenchies wearing "badger" collars. **5.** In the style of Fabergé, this gold-mounted crystal and bejeweled "surprise egg" hides a French Bulldog when closed. It was made by German artist Emil Becker. **6.** Surprisingly, very few French Bulldog collectibles were made in France. This very fine enameled clock is marked Brevette, France and dates from the 1920s. **7.** A superb German silver and enamel antique brooch decorated with marcasites and rubies for the eyes. **8.** A rare demi-lune-shaped clock is enameled with two French Bulldogs after a painting by Austrian artist Emil Herz. **9.** A finely carved smoky crystal Frenchie with gold and rose diamond eyes is attributed to the Fabergé Workshop.

Car Mascots

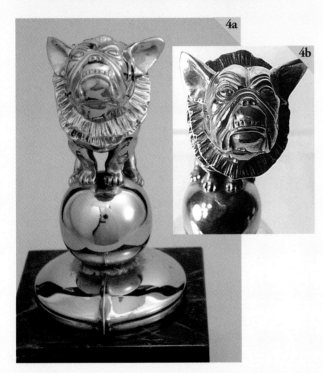

1. A superb silvered bronze hood ornament is signed A. Delm and dates from 1920s France. This large mascot is surely one of the greatest French Bulldog bronzes. 2. A Cubist ruff-collared Frenchie hood ornament is a silvered bronze Art Deco masterwork. 3. A 1934 French advertisement for Goodrich tires is captioned "robust and supple like a Bulldog." 4a. Wearing an elaborate "badger" collar, this Frenchie is one of the finest car mascots. This model is made of chromed bronze but there also exists a signed deluxe version in silvered bronze with the Frenchie standing on an ivory ball. It was produced by the French firm Cardeilhac in the 1920s. 4b. Detail of mascot. 5. *The Beauty and the Beast* is a patinated bronze car mascot known as *La Rennomée* or *The Renowned*. She is an allegorical divinity who sounds trumpets of fame to all humanity. 6. A very fine and expressive bronze hood ornament signed by French sculptor Gaston Bourcart dates from the 1920s. This is yet another French Bulldog bronze masterpiece. 7a. A Cubist model of a chained Frenchie is by éditions Marvel and was a large production. It dates from the 1920s. 7b. This amusing grinning Frenchie is Marvel's non-Cubist version and quite a rarity.

The French Bulldog

Porcelains

1. The brindle-colored French Bulldog is not often seen in porcelain as the coloring is so hard to imitate. This magnificent model by Elgersburg, Germany is signed by artist Dorothea Moldenhauer and dates from before 1919. She also sculpted this model in miniature as a pied for Rosenthal. **2.** An enormous and exceptional pair of pieds with glass eyes and huge "bat ears" is by the Wiener Werkstätte and a great rarity. **3.** The pied on the left is by the Czechoslovakian firm Amphora and has a hallmark dating from 1918–39. The fawn is from the same mold but by the Eichwalder Factory, Bohemia, circa 1945. As it was a fairly common practice for artists to keep their molds, this possibly explains the phenomenon of this duo. **4.** An unusual bisque fawn with painted details was made in Germany in the 1930s. **5.** By the Wiener Werkstätte, these rather serious-looking Frenchies are from the same mold but with different coloring and character. Each has an elaborate studded collar glazed in red and blue. **6.** Enough to give any collector "Frenchie fever," these superb whelps with oversized paws and tummies swollen with milk were designed by Konrad Schmid for Nymphenburg in 1928. The model initially came in three sizes but the size in between the two illustrated above was discontinued in the 1940s for unknown reasons. **7.** A very creative Art Deco Frenchie by Royal Dux, Bohemia. **8.** Two of the most expressive Frenchies in porcelain. The fawn on the left is by Goebel and dates from about 1920. The superb pied is by Augarten and has the famous blue "beehive" mark from 1922–30. **9 a–c.** An exquisite pair of Frenchies on a plinth by Ens, Germany with a hallmark from before 1919. Each was also modeled separately. **9d.** This standing Frenchie is a later copy of the standing Ens Frenchie but in reverse. It is by the Czech manufacturer Johann Maresch. **10.** While all three of these very refined models are from the same mold, they have quite different coloring and demeanor. Manufactured by Heubach, Germany, all are signed Fischer and the one on a pedestal is dated 1911.

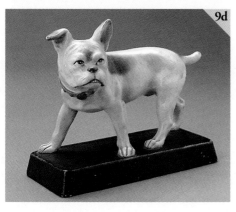

11. Two classical masterworks decorated in pale green, gray and ochre are among the most beautiful and detailed Frenchies ever produced. By Hutschenreuther, Germany, they have a hallmark from 1920. 12. With ears up and tons of personality, this huge Frenchie from 1930s Germany has it all! 13 a–b. *Tommy* is a very rare documentary Art Nouveau porcelain by Fraureuth. His name appears on the front of the plinth and on top it is signed R. König and dated 1919. The white model was a larger production than the brindle, which is very difficult to find. 14. This remarkable large porcelain by Rosenthal dates from 1912 and is signed Gsell. Both Pierrot and his Frenchie have ruffed clown collars. 15. A perfect example of Victoriana, this elaborate terracotta damsel on a promenade with her Frenchie is signed G. Lamipiroti and marked on the base "Made in Italy." 16. Erich Hoesel designed several French Bulldog models for Meissen, some of which are still in production today. This scarce and elegant pair dates from 1921. 17. Two perfect examples of "humanized" dogs are these German porcelains. One taps the drums and the other is preparing for Wimbledon. 18. A huge Frenchie, either German or Czech, is a perfect Art Deco Casanova. He is "dressed to the nines" and ready to go out on the prowl. 19. A masterpiece by Lauritz Jensen, this superb Royal Copenhagen "tiger" brindle dates from before 1913 and has been out of production for decades. This Frenchie was also decorated as a pied, and both models reflect the earlier and more slender breed style. 20. An absolutely charming early Art Deco Frenchie with enormous ears is by Heubach and signed by Roland Paris, who made several other models for this factory. 21. One of the best porcelains from Japan, this Frenchie from the 1940s is a planter with huge "rabbit" ears. It copies an earlier German model. 22. A delicate and original classical French Bulldog is by Galluba & Hoffmann. This extremely rare model dates from 1910. 23. A high-quality Cubist porcelain Frenchie by Sitzendorf looks to have been designed by Picasso. It is in fact a toothbrush holder with a slot on top of the Frenchie's head into which the toothbrush is inserted vertically.

The French Bulldog

24. This black-masked fawn on a pedestal by the Thuringian manufacturer Aelteste Volkstedter is one of the earliest recorded Frenchies and bears a mark from 1880-1890. The smaller model is a copy by the Heinz Schaubach Factory and dates from 1940-1962. 25. A trio of caricatured fawn pups with "googly" eyes appear to be racing toward the dinner bowl, especially the middle one with his tongue sticking out of his mouth! This rare and complicated sculpture is by the Wiener Werkstätte. 26. Considered one of the great masterpieces of dog sculpture, this superb life-size French Bulldog was originally produced on a pillow with four tassels. It was designed by Maria-Theresia Ernst for the German firm Nymphenburg in 1917. Just one month later, probably due to high production costs, it was made without the pillow. Nymphenburg is much admired for its sparkling jewel-like glazes and remarkable attention to details. 27. Revealing a very unique expression, this monumental Frenchie from Czechoslovakia circa 1920 is one of the largest of all porcelain Frenchies. 28. An unusual large seated Frenchie dates from 1940s Japan. 29. A large pied Frenchie pup with a yellow "leather" collar is probably Czech or German. This rare and refined piece is from the first quarter of the 20th century. 30. A brilliantly decorated pair of early Art Deco Frenchies are signed Herkner and were made during Goldscheider's best period (1926-1938).

Pieces de Résistance

Lamps

1a. Three comic perfume lamps by Graefenthal & Heinz, Germany. All are from the same mold and share the same model number though they are most different in glazing and expression. They date from the late 1930s. **1b.** Lamps lit. **2a.** An elegant perfume lamp as a Frenchie wearing a badger collar and standing over a cord of wood dates from 1930s Germany. **2b.** Lamp lit. **3.** One of the great lamps, this superb Art Deco model is by Galluba & Hoffmann, Germany. **4.** Goebel produced several perfume lamps modeled after such Disney characters as Pluto and Donald Duck. This "cartoonesque" Art Deco perfume lamp looks to have been inspired by Walt himself! **5.** The rarest of the perfume lamps, this pair is from the same mold but with very different glazing and expressions. Their "badger" collars are remarkable for the details. **6.** This unusual lamp is a transitional piece. While the gilt brass base is pure Art Nouveau, the frosted glass Frenchie head is stylized and very much early Art Deco. **7.** This sullen-looking Frenchie with great ears is a large lamp by Sitzendorf, Germany and dates from the 1920s. **8.** A rare miniature Cubist Czech lamp is only four inches tall and dates from the 1930s.

The French Bulldog

Tableware

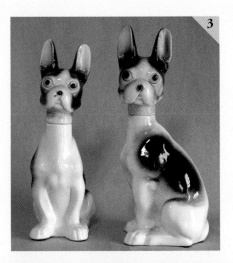

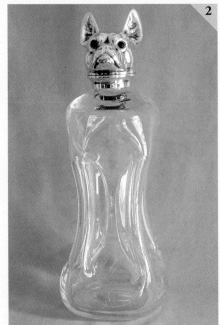

1. A hard-to-find 1930s German teapot in the form of a Frenchie with an elaborate collar and great ears. **2.** This large Art Nouveau decanter from Austria with a silver Frenchie head as the stopper is a great work of art. It appears as though the "legs" were made separately but, remarkably, all of it was blown from a single piece of glass. **3.** A very creative pair of decanters, elongated and rather the opposite of a Frenchie, by Goebel and dating from the 1930s. **4.** A Frenchie in the form of a wooden peppermill with glass eyes is by Marlux, France. This amusing piece dates from 1930–1940. **5.** A charming Frenchie napkin ring dates from 1930s Germany. **6.** By Pfeffer Gotha, Germany, this mustard pot is a "must have" for the dinner table! **7.** A rare amethyst and rose quartz servant-caller. Probably of Austrian origin, it dates from the early 20th century. When you push the Frenchie head, it rings to let the kitchen staff know that it is time to clear the table or move on to the next course. Most of these bell-ringers were made of bronze and were "toys" of the wealthy. **8.** An Art Deco child's warming bowl is enameled with a Frenchie's head. This unique piece has a funnel at the top into which warm water is poured, which then flows into a channel that surrounds the dish to keep the baby's food warm. **9.** A Vienna gilt bronze bell-push of a French Bulldog with an ivory "bone." When pressed, it chimes a bell in the kitchen to let the servants know that they are needed. Signed by Austrian master Friedrich Gornik, it was cast around the beginning of the 20th century. **10.** A Frenchie confronts a frog while a rooster watches the upcoming drama on this 1920s deep plate by Villeroy & Boch. **11.** A superb silver candlestick by Louis Comfort Tiffany dates from 1910–1920. **12.** A silver and mahogany tea tray lined with French Bull Dog Club of America bronze medals is by Reed & Barton and was commissioned by Arnold Lawson of the Noswal Kennels to commemorate his wins. **13.** Two little boys sit on a divan playing with their Frenchie in this remarkable early 20th century German gilt porcelain. Surprisingly, the top lifts off to reveal that it is a candy box.

The French Bulldog

Desk Accessories

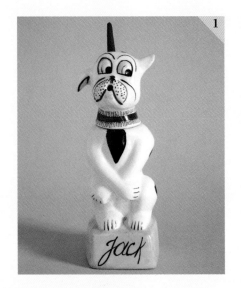

1. Jack, with his "googly" eyes and "badger" collar, is a rare inkwell from 1930s Germany. **2.** A boldly decorated Art Deco German porcelain is a stamp-wetter. Just moisten the sponge and no need to lick! **3.** An amusing clock with revolving glass eyes that show the hours and minutes is very hard to find in working condition. Made in Germany, it dates from the 1930s. **4a–b.** A magnificent personal seal of Edward, Duke of Windsor, is gilt silver and ivory decorated with rubies and tourmalines. It has the crowned monogram "E" on the seal surface, and the finial is in the form of a French Bulldog head. Edward and Wallis were well known for their love of Pugs, so this Frenchie seal is a bit of a mystery although the Duchess had a pet Frenchie as a child. **5.** A very expressive pair of harlequins playing mandolins has ruff-collared howling Frenchies at their feet. This pair of bookends by Kronheim & Oldenberg is made of brass-finished spelter with enameled details and dated 1936. **6.** One of a pair of large porcelain bookends by Bing & Grondahl, Denmark. Its mate probably tumbled off a bookshelf decades ago. At first glance the function is not obvious, but the back is completely flat. This is a top-quality piece signed by Sophus Jensen-Kromand, who worked for B&G from 1920–1947.

Toys

1a. Poor "Swipes," as his tag reads, has been in a scrape. This rare vintage German velveteen with glass tears squeaks when his belly is pushed. **1b.** This Frenchie from the German children's book *Bully und Mini* bears a strong resemblance to Swipes on this page . **2.** A rare trio of plush children's toys with glass eyes, painted details and traditional ruff collars were made in Germany circa 1930. The brown Frenchie is larger than life at an astounding 20 inches! **3.** One of the most extraordinary toys, this large Austrian velveteen dates from about 1910 and has glass eyes, a wax nose, two visible teeth and a very detailed collar. **4.** The German firm Steiff made thousands of Frenchies. This standing version on wheels in the form of a pull toy is quite rare and dates from the 1920s. **5.** A celluloid baby rattle by Irwin USA dates from the 1930s. With his grimace, one might wonder if he would frighten a child! **6.** An Art Deco wooden toy was apparently much loved, as both ears have been nibbled on. **7.** "Bully" is a tin lithographed wind-up toy marked Made in Germany, US Zone, and manufactured by the Lehmann Co. He is a wonderful post-WWII mechanical toy and hard to find with the original box. **8.** One serious-looking Frenchie toy and another quite hilarious one, which has a message on its belly to "press me." After doing so, he squeaks! Both are made of celluloid and date from the 1930s.

The French Bulldog

Sculptures

1. Trained as a sculptress but a famous breeder of Boxers, Friederun von Miram-Stockmann created one of the greatest French Bulldog masterpieces. This bronze of a Frenchie staring down a bullfrog had a record sale at the Munich Glass Palace in 1913. This is the only known example and it has been speculated that others were melted down for ammunition during WWI. **2a.** This Frenchie, who must be convinced he is a large dog, appears to be reining in a stallion in this wonderful bronze signed by Sicilian sculptor Michele Auteri-Pomar. It dates from the first quarter of the 20th century. **2b.** Detail of the Frenchie in the sculpture. **3.** An outstanding patinated bronze of three Frenchies is signed Hugo Klingseisen and probably dates from the first quarter of the 20th century. **4.** A large and superbly carved wooden Frenchie with painted details and a metal-studded collar is quite similar to several 1920s miniature Austrian bronzes. **5a.** Fritz Diller was a famous "animalier" who made 21 porcelain dogs for the German firm Rosenthal. He produced this extraordinary version in silvered metal about 1913 for the German manufacturer WMF, which was famous for its silvered Art Nouveau objects. Each dog is signed and was also made separately just like their porcelain counterparts. **5b.** Detail of the Diller porcelain pair by Rosenthal. **6.** A superb bronze signed Stundl and dated 1913 is slender and elegant, much like the Frenchies at the beginning of the 20th century. **7.** A late 19th-century bronze French Bulldog is signed on the base C. CHARLES, who was a listed French scupltor. This detailed Frenchie is also marked Louchet, which was a Paris foundry where the finishing work was completed. **8.** A very original painted wood Cubist sculpture with a vessel to perhaps hold cigarettes. **9a.** A fine gilt bronze begging Frenchie circa 1910. **9b.** A rare Frenchie that copies this bronze is by the Wiener Werkstätte and quite original with its polka-dot pillow. **10.** A terracotta model of a Frenchie and a turtle by Emile Rouff.

Tobacciana

1. Two versions of a very unusual Art Deco pipe rest are by Goebel, Germany, circa 1930. **2.** A pair of comical humidors that captures everything Frenchie was made in Germany in the 1930s. **3.** This hilarious Art Deco matchsafe with glass eyes has most of its original paint. It never fails to make one smile. **4.** An imposing and finely carved wooden humidor with great ears and glass eyes dates from 1930s Germany. The hinged head swings back to reveal a reservoir for loose tobacco. **5.** The ultimate in refined kitsch, this remarkable wooden matchsafe is probably German or Austrian circa 1920. There is a lid on the dog's back, which, when opened, reveals a compartment for cigarettes or matches. The "collar" has holes to be fitted with wooden matches, which amusingly imitates a "badger" collar. **6.** A small wooden Frenchie from Germany with red glass eyes is a lighter and hard to find in decent condition. **7.** A Cubist Frenchie ashtray from Czechoslovakia is made of spelter and has glass eyes. The glass bowl on top is original to the piece and hard to come by. **8.** A superb silver-enameled cigarette case is Austrian and dates from about 1920. **9.** A very fine silver-enameled cigarette case with a lovely pied Frenchie painted in a soft palette is Austrian and dates from the 1920s.

Posters, Paintings and Paper

1. A page from the 1927 German children's book *Bully und Mini* where both are eagerly awaiting "un bon repas!" 2. A rare early 20th century Austrian poster advertising furs. 3. A gouache of a brindle with perfect "bat" ears is by French painter Anna Bellet-Laquère, who exhibited at the Parisian salons from 1910-1934. 4. A 1928 Swiss lithograph poster advertising a dog show in Lucerne is by famous poster artist Otto Landolt (1889-1951). 5. A lovely pastel by French artist André Margat (1903-1999) 6. A 1920s advertising sign for Santo, a vacuum-cleaning service in existence at a time when vacuums were too expensive for most to own. The business ended after WWII, and this is the only sign known to exist. 7. A beautifully rendered pastel signed Glatz and dated 1933. 8. A vintage postcard of a Frenchie wearing a "badger" collar. 9. A photo of Colette and her Frenchies from 1907. She is perhaps best known for her 1944 novel *Gigi*. It was made into a very successful Hollywood film starring Maurice Chevalier, Louis Jourdan and Leslie Caron. 10. A great vintage Valentine card from 1920s Germany. 11. A hilarious New Year's postcard of a ruff-collared Frenchie holding a horseshoe and smoking a cigarette. On his cap is a four-leaf clover, whose leaves, according to legend, symbolize hope, faith, love and luck. 12. Fritz is the ultimate "humanized" Frenchie. He is ready to do battle for the Kaiser. 13. A gorgeous postcard by the Wiener Werkstätte is signed by Mela Koehler. 14. Painted in 1970 by artist Josepha von Furstenberg is a portrait of one of the famous Ratibor French Bullies.

"FRITZ,"—A GERMAN WAR DOG

Bonne Année

Paris 12. Junio 1914.

The French Bulldog

Miscellaneous Remarkable Frenchie Collectibles

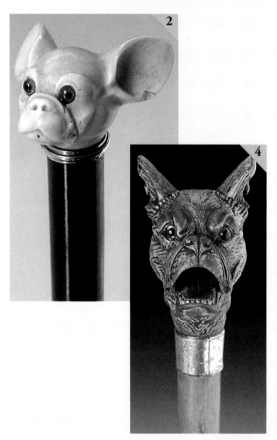

1a. This exquisite ladies' fan is from the famous Sacher Hotel and Restaurant in Vienna. It dates from circa 1920 and was handed out to the female guests on hot summer days. **1b.** A rare postcard written by Anna Sacher with an image of her Frenchies. She writes: "I am thanking you for the beautiful flowers, and do hope you will be well able to use the knowledge you acquired from me in your own house. Best Regards, Anna Sacher." **2.** A fine ivory cane head with glass eyes comes from Austria circa 1920. **3.** A rare Austrian velveteen Frenchie as a compact for face powder. **4.** A finely carved wooden cane head is from early 20th-century Austria. **5.** A rare wooden tape measure with glass eyes copies a silver decanter head from Austria. **6.** A sensational child's umbrella from 1920s Germany is probably from the famous manufacturer Bernhard Hermann. **7.** A brass Art Deco door knocker made in Great Britain in the 1930s. **8.** Very few Frenchie collectibles were made in America. This large doorstop is by the Fulper Art Pottery Company and dates from 1920–1930. **9.** Frenchie kitsch is at its best in this amazing pair of children's slippers with the original box. Each slipper is marked "Bavaria." **10 a–d.** A superb early 20th century Austrian silver-enameled lady's opera purse has an onyx push-button. When the button is depressed, the purse opens to reveal a mirror and compartments for coins, rouge and even a few cigarettes.

5

6

7

8

9

10a

10b

10c

10d

Dean Wolstenholme, English, 1798–1882; *A French Bulldog*; Oil on canvas, 14 x 18 inches; Private collection; Photograph courtesy William Secord Gallery, New York.

A Visit to
LA GALERIE
du French Bulldog

By William Secord

While the dog has appeared in various art forms since at least the Babylonian times, it was only in the mid-19th century that dogs truly came into their own. With the leadership of Queen Victoria and the royal family, a wealthy middle class and the evolution of organized dog shows, dogs enjoyed an unprecedented popularity as the subject matter for fine sculptors and painters.

This evolution of 19th- and early 20th-century dog painting was in many ways mirrored by the evolution of a very special breed: the French Bulldog. Believed to have originated in England, where it was known as the Miniature Bulldog or Toy Bulldog, the French Bulldog as we know it evolved as a breed in the late 19th century, at a time when it was fashionable to have one's dog painted by a prominent artist of the day. While the artist Sir Edwin Landseer reigned supreme in the mid-19th century, artists such as Maud Earl, Fannie Moody and Arthur Wardle created an extraordinary visual record of the prominent purebred dogs of the late 19th century, including the French Bulldog.

One of the earliest depictions of the French Bulldog type is by Dean Wolstenholme, Jr. (1798–1882), an English artist who specialized in painting horses and animals. While the painting is not dated, it is safe to conjecture that it was painted in England before 1880. While it depicts a dog with much less bone and substance than later examples, it does have the characteristic bat ears so typical of the modern breed.

The popular small bulldogs of England soon gained great favor in France in the mid-19th century. Although they were not actively shown, they became popular as pets, first with entertainers and streetwalkers and then with the fashionable ladies of Parisian society. These dogs were depicted in paintings as early as the 1870s, and one

The French Bulldog

fanciers became more organized in France, holding regular meetings and in 1885 creating a provisional registry for the breed. A French breed club was established with Marcel Rogers as its first president in 1888, combining with another breed club in 1898 to create the Club du Bouledogue Français.

Auguste Vimar must have been a great friend of the breed, for it is further honored with his painting titled *The Conoisseurs,* circa 1885. Painted in a similar tonal range to the Vimar in the Marseilles Museum, it depicts four dogs and a monkey admiring a portrait of a white French Bulldog, mounted on an easel. The subject of the portrait sits in the lower left, looking up at its likeness, seemingly to determine whether the artist has captured his true likeness. The practice of attributing human feelings to animals, or anthropomorphism, had been popularized earlier in the 19th century by the British artist Sir Edwin Landseer, animal painter to Queen Victoria. Indeed, the Royal Collection has a painting titled *The Conoisseurs,* in which Landseer's dogs,

sometimes sees them depicted as ladies' companions in paintings by such great French artists as Toulouse-Lautrec, himself from an aristocratic family.

One of the first dated French paintings of a French Bulldog is in the Musée des Beaux Arts in Marseilles. Painted by Auguste Vimar (1851–1916), *Causerie des Chiens,* translated literally as "gossiping dogs," shows a fawn French Bulldog at the apex of a pyramidal composition of other dogs: a toy spaniel, a terrier and a large hound. The French Bulldog is clearly the alpha dog of the family and sits overseeing his charges with an almost haughty expression. It was in the 1880s that French Bulldog became

Above, top: Auguste Vimar, French, 1815-1916; *Causerie des Chiens,* 1885; Oil on canvas, 36¾ x 35 inches; Collection Musée des Beaux Arts, Marseilles.

Above, bottom: Auguste Vimar, French, 1851-1916; *The Conoisseurs*; Oil on canvas, 23 x 31¼ inches; Collection Jayne and Greg Sidwell; Photograph courtesy William Secord Gallery, New York.

Facing page, top left: A. V. A. Boudarel, French, 19th century; *Mastiff with French Bulldog*; Bronze, 11½ x 8 x 10¾ inches; Collection The American Kennel Club Museum of the Dog, gift of Marie A. Moore.

Facing page, top right: Richard Fath, French, 1900-1952; *Standing French Bulldog With Head Turned*; Original plaster study, signed, 6½ x 5½ x 2¾ inches; Private collection; Photograph courtesy William Secord Gallery, New York.

Facing page, bottom: Richard Fath, French, 1900-1952; *French Bulldog Head Study*; Terracotta, signed, 4½ inches; Private collection; Photograph courtesy William Secord Gallery, New York.

A Visit to la Galerie du French Bulldog

The French Bulldog, or Bouledogue Francais, as it was known in Paris in the late 1800s, had come a very long way from its humble origins as an English immigrant. In a few short decades the high society of Paris had taken the breed under its wing, and there are many stories of the breed's accompanying ladies of high birth. Indeed, it was around this time that the Prince of Wales, later King Edward VII, became known for his French Bulldogs, which

Lassie and Myrtle, look over the artist's shoulder as if to criticize his work. It is probable that the dogs in Vimar's painting are his own dogs, and like Landseer before him, he trusts their opinions enough to have them criticize his work.

French sculptors as well as painters chose this charming breed as their subject matter, and the American Kennel Club Museum of the Dog has an endearing portrait of a Mastiff with a French Bulldog by A. V. A. Boudarel (French, 19th century). The Mastiff sits firmly on the ground, while the Frenchie looks up at him in a gesture of companionship. Richard Fath (1900–1952), who worked in the early 20th century, was of more importance for French Bulldog fanciers, however, for he prided himself on sculpting purebred dogs exactly as they looked. His one-of-a-kind plaster study, *Standing French Bulldog With Head Turned,* is a good example of his work, but he also did many smaller pieces, including a terracotta medallion of a Frenchie head, which is particularly well done.

The French Bulldog

It was also around this time that the Prince of Wales was photographed at Balmoral with Peter's offspring, Paul, in September of 1899. Both Peter and Paul would probably have been considered Toy Bulldogs, although they were clearly what we know

in England at the time would have been called Toy Bulldogs. His first well-known dog was Peter, portrayed in a watercolor miniature by Gertrude Massey. It is a tribute to the prince's affection for the dog that Massey did the watercolor, for she was well known for her miniature portraits of the royal family, including the Prince of Wales when he was a young boy.

Above, left: Gertrude Massey, English, 20th century; *Peter, King Edward VII's French Bulldog;* Watercolor on ivory; Courtesy Bonham's, London.

Above, right: Thomas Fall, English, 20th century; *Prince Albert, Prince of Wales, with Paul, at Balmoral,* September 1899; Photograph courtesy Mary Evans Picture Library.

Facing page, top left: Maud Earl, English, 1864-1943; *England Expects (Champion "Peter Amos" and Champion "Ninon de l'Enclos"),* large detail; Owned by the Lady Kathleen Pilkington; Collection The Kennel Club, London.

Facing page, top right: Maud Earl, English, 1864-1943; *The French Bulldog Ch. Qui Qui of Amersham,* large detail, 1913; Owned by Mrs. Pelham Clinton; Photogravure, 12½ x 11¼ inches; Collection The Kennel Club, London.

Facing page, bottom left: Maud Earl, English, 1864-1943; *Standing French Bulldog, 1910;* Oil on canvas, 18 x 24 inches; The E. M. Hershey II Collection; Photograph courtesy William Secord Gallery, New York.

Facing page, bottom right: Maud Earl, English, 1864-1943; *The French Bulldog, Ch. Dinette,* large detail, 1913; Owned by Mrs. Charles Waterlow; Photogravure, 11¼ x 12½ inches; Collection William Secord Gallery, Inc., New York.

of today as French Bulldogs. It is notable that they both had bat ears, which would imply that they were French imports, as the rose ear was preferred over the bat ear by the English Toy Bulldog breeders of the day. Dogs imported from France during this period were first shown in the Toy Group. In 1905, after the founding of the French Bulldog Club of England in 1902, The Kennel Club allowed French Bulldogs to be shown as a separate breed, but as a variety of foreign dogs, under the name "Bouledogue Français."

It was around the turn of the century that, as with the French Bulldog in France, the Toy Bulldog reached a greater popularity with the English titled classes. Two dogs owned by Lady Pilkington, one of the founders of the Toy Bulldog Club, were depicted by Maud Earl in a painting now at The Kennel Club office in London: *England Expects (Champion "Peter Amos" and Champion "Ninon de l'Enclos")*. Painted in Maud Earl's signature style of the period, it clearly

depicts Ch. Peter Amos with erect bat ears. Peter Amos became a great winner in the show ring, but it was around this time that bat-eared Toy Bulldogs were almost entirely superseded by rose-eared specimens. While we do not know the identity of the French Bulldog portrayed in Maud Earl's portrait of 1910, it was undoubtedly a well-known dog of the day. Earl continued to paint other French Bulldogs from well-known kennels. A portrait of Ch. Qui Qui of Amersham, painted around 1913, was reproduced

The French Bulldog

painting from the same portfolio is *The French Bulldog, Ch. Dinette,* owned by Mrs. Charles Waterlow. The whereabouts of the originals of both paintings are unknown, but we are fortunate in having the photogravures from the portfolio as a record of how they looked.

Mr W.W. CROCKER'S FRENCH BULLDOG "PARISIANA"

LADY LEWIS' "HAMPTON PUCK"

in black and white as one of the plates in her now-rare portfolio *Whose Dog Art Thou?* It is painted in Earl's characteristic style, with the dog in great detail and the background very loosely rendered. Its title, *The French Bulldog Ch. Qui Qui of Amersham,* clearly identifies the breed, and the dog was eventually exported to America. Another French Bulldog

Above, left: Maud Earl, English, 1864-1943; *King Edward's Bulls;* Casein on silk, 48 x 24 inches; The E. M. Hershey II Collection; Photograph courtesy William Secord Gallery, New York.
Above, right: Arthur Wardle, English, 1864-1949; *Prominent Dogs,* circa 1895; Gouache on paper, 16½ x 10½ inches; Private collection; Photograph courtesy Sara Davenport Fine Paintings.
Facing page, top left: Fannie Moody, English, circa 1861-circa 1947; *Entente Cordiale;* Oil on canvas, 18 x 15½ inches; Collection The Kennel Club, London.
Facing page, top right: Florence Mabel Hollams, English, 1877-1963; *Buzzy, a French Bulldog;* Oil on panel, 14 x 15 inches; The E. M. Hershey II Collection; Photograph courtesy William Secord Gallery, New York.
Facing page, bottom left: Herbert Dicksee, English, 1862-1942; *Sleeping French Bulldog;* Etching, 2¼ x 6¼ inches; Collection The American Kennel Club Museum of the Dog, gift of Zellah B. Hilton.
Facing page, bottom right: Carl Reichert, Austrian; *French Bulldog, 1874;* Oil on canvas, 15½ x 12¼ inches; Collection The American Kennel Club.

received a prize for modeling. Maud Earl matured as an artist when the purebred dog—both as a pet and in the show ring—had reached an unprecedented popularity, and purebred dog fanciers soon came to rely on her to paint portraits of their favorites. She was a prolific artist, and she painted innumerable purebred dogs. Moreover, she painted

The name Maud Earl became virtually synonymous with paintings of purebred dogs, and she painted a relatively great number of French Bulldogs in her long career, many for prominent dog fanciers of the day. Indeed, it was her association with royalty that was to give Maud Earl an added cachet. She painted for Queen Victoria, as well as for the queen's son, Edward VII. Maud Earl was born in 1864, the daughter of the well-known dog and animal painter George Earl (1824–1908) and the niece of the artist Thomas Earl (19th century). First taught by her father, she had little formal training, and she later attended the Royal Female School of Art, where she

The French Bulldog

Luska, his Wire Fox Terrier Caesar and Princess Alexandra's Borzoi Alex.

While no portraits by Maud Earl of King Edward's Peter and Paul are known, she did complete a portrait of three of the king's French Bulldogs, titled *King Edward's Bulls*, but they are dated 1927, some 17 years after the king's death. Maud Earl had emigrated to America around 1915, where she continued her success as an animal painter. Working for some of the most prominent dog fanciers of the day, she developed a new style of painting, greatly influenced by Japanese art. She often painted on silk, in what she referred to as decorative panels. *King Edward's Bulls*, portraying one dark brindle and two fawn French Bulldogs, is painted in this style. The dogs appear in a type of Oriental landscape, looking off to the left as if waiting for their master.

them from life, rather than with the use of photographs. She would pose the dog on a portable stool with casters, then move the stool so as to get the best pose and lighting, without disturbing the dog. A single portrait might take as little as two days, working from about 10 a.m. to 4 p.m.

Maud Earl's works soon came to the attention of the royal family, when she was summoned to Windsor Castle to paint Queen Victoria's white Collie, Snowball. Victoria was a great animal lover, and in the late 19th century, Sir Edwin Landseer, Gourlay Steell, Freiderich Keyl and others were commissioned to paint portraits of her dogs. It was a great honor for Maud Earl to have her as a patron. Other members of the royal family came to use her services as well, and the Prince of Wales, later Edward VII, commissioned her to paint portraits of his Siberian Sledge dog

Above, top: P. Kapell, German, 20th century; *Standing French Bulldog,* 1928; Oil on canvas, 21¼ x 26 inches; Private collection; Photograph courtesy William Secord Gallery, New York.
Above, bottom: Alexander Pope, American, 1849-1924; *La Belle Wanda,* December 1917; Oil on canvas, 24 x 28 inches; The E. M. Hershey II Collection; Photograph courtesy William Secord Gallery, New York.
Facing page, top: S. Raphael, American, 20th century; *French Bulldog;* Oil on canvas, 21 x 24 inches; Collection The American Kennel Club.
Facing page, bottom: Fred Sitzler, American, 20th century; *Ch. Le Petit Marquis de La France II,* 1954; Oil on board, 14 x 16 inches; Private collection; Photograph courtesy William Secord Gallery, New York.

Many other British artists painted the French Bulldog, including the famous Arthur Wardle (1864–1949) and others such as Herbert Dicksee (1862–1942), Fannie Moody (circa 1861–circa 1947) and Frances Mabel Hollams (1877–1963). Wardle excelled at painting animals, and dogs in particular. He evidently had little formal training, but he studied animals at the London Zoo and was a regular visitor to dog shows. Wardle was equally proficient in oil, watercolor and pastel, and he became a member of the Pastel Society in 1911 and the Royal Society of Painters in Watercolor in 1922. His pastel of Princess Alexandra's Peter, seemingly unrelated to her husband's more famous dog, is from one of his sketch books. Wardle's study of royal dogs, which included the King's Clumber Spaniel Sandringham Boss, also includes studies of two French Bulldogs, identified as W. W. Crocker's Parisiana and Lady Lewis's Harpton Puck. Lady Lewis, proprietress of the Harpton kennels, had both Toy Bulldogs and French Bulldogs.

Her first dog, Harpton Floss, became a champion and was under 21 pounds.

Other depictions by British artists include the intimate portrait of a Bulldog and a French Bulldog by Fannie Moody. The artist often painted portraits of similar breeds in the same painting, in this case showing the French Bulldog with one of its ancestors. The well-known artist Herbert Dicksee (English, 1862–1942) also did a number of French Bulldogs, including the sleeping puppy now in the American Kennel Club Museum of the Dog.

Depictions of French Bulldogs were not restricted, however, to England and France, as there were active breeders in many other European countries as well as in America. Carl Reichert's portrait of a white ancestor of our present-day Frenchie, dated 1874, is an especially early example. Known for his small-scale paintings of dogs and cats, Reichert painted with an academic realism in small, tightly controlled brush strokes. A sophisticated artist, he studied in Gretz, Munich and later in Rome. He was known as a genre and animal painter, and we can only assume that this dog would have been painted in Austria, rather than on his travels. The first Toy Bulldogs were imported

The French Bulldog

into Austria between 1870 and 1890, but it was not until Prince Coburg brought a white dog named Snob back to Austria and others began to import dogs on a more regular basis that a breed club was founded (in 1898).

French Bulldogs were also known in Germany around the same time. P. Kapell's painting of a dark brindle dog, dated 1928, is much later and is done in an impressionistic style. It wears a boar-bristle collar, so characteristic of the breed; this type of collar was said by some to tickle the backs of the ears so as to encourage them to stay erect.

It was in the United States, however, that the French Bulldog was to achieve even greater popularity than in Europe, with American fanciers importing Frenchies from France in great numbers. Considering the popularity of the breed in the early years of the 20th century, it is surprising that so few paintings of French Bulldogs remain. Alexander Pope (1849–1924) started his career as a portrait painter, but soon came to specialize in painting animals, especially dogs. Almost entirely self-taught, he spent many hours studying animals in the zoological gardens of New York. He was very active in the sporting world around the turn of the century and published two portfolios of prints: *Upland Game Birds and Water Fowls* and *Celebrated Dogs of America*. His 1917 portrait of La Belle Wanda was commissioned by her breeder, John B. Fox. She won Reserve Winners

Above: Christine Merrill, Contemporary American; *Ch. Razzamatazz*, 2006; Oil on board, 16 x 18 inches; Collection Jayne and Greg Sidwell; Photograph courtesy William Secord Gallery, New York.
Facing page: Charlotte Sorré, Contemporary American; *Oreo, Popcorn and Licorice;* Oil on canvas, 18 x 26 inches; The E. M. Hershey II Collection; Photograph courtesy William Secord Gallery, New York.

Bitch at the New York French Bulldog specialty show of 1916. Other American paintings of French Bulldogs include S. Raphael's undated portrait and Fred Sitzler's portrait of Ch. Petit Marquis de la France II from 1954.

Modern artists, working in an academic tradition, have more recently taken up the breed, and several fine contemporary artists have created paintings in the 19th-century tradition. Charlotte Sorré, a New York artist, recently painted an engaging portrait of Mr. E. M. Hershey's three French Bulldogs, Oreo, Popcorn and Licorice. Constance Payne, from near Buffalo, New York, works more in the French tradition of the great 19th-century painter Rosa Bonheur, and her head study of Ch. Hollycroft's Going Supersonic is executed with an atmospheric painterly brush stroke. Christine Merrill's portrait of Ch. Razzamatazz is in the 18th-century English academic tradition, where the dog's image is rendered with great attention to detail, creating a highly finished surface.

While the heyday of dog paintings was no doubt in the mid- to late 19th century, there has during the past ten years been a resurgence of interest in animal paintings, and dog paintings in particular. Realistic painters such as Sir Edwin Landseer and John Emms fell out of favor in the mid-20th century, but with a renewed interest in realistic painting, and a more heterogeneous art world where abstract painting can easily coexist with more realistic works, there has been a renewed interest in dog paintings. It is fortunate for today's French Bulldog fanciers that many new artists are coming to the fore who can visually depict the French Bulldogs of today, both our show dogs and our beloved pets.

The French Bulldog

Above: Constance Payne, Contemporary American; *Ch. Hollycroft's Going Supersonic;* Oil on panel, 12 x 9 inches; Private collection; Photograph courtesy William Secord Gallery, New York.
Facing page: Contemporary American painter and Frenchie lover Constance Payne with her little angel Gus, formally Oh Gustav Mon Ange Jalee. Gus was bred by Jan Ginther of Jalee Frenchies; his sire was Ch. LeBull's Elwood, and his great-grandfather was the famous Ch. LeBull's Fargo, owned by Arlie Alford.

APPENDIX I
Top-Producing Stud Dogs

Every effort has been made to ensure the accuracy of these records, but an occasional error or omission may have crept in and we apologize for that. The records, as recorded and published by the American Kennel Club and published in the books by Camino Books, Inc., are as follows for top-producing stud dogs through February 2006:

Ch. Cox's Goodtime Charlie Brown............97
Ch. Cox's Goodtime Ace In The Hole ex Ch Cox's Goodtime Mindy Lou of K 'n D

Ch. C and D's Laboss Mon Buntin................52
Ch. Cox's Goodtime Polar Bear ex Ch. C and D's Madonna LaMon

Ch. Bandog's One In A Million.....................36
Ch. K and D Foxy Joe of Cox's Goodtime ex Ch. Bandog's Joy to the World

Ch. Hampton's Chevalier...............................30
Ch. Terrette's Tourbillon D'Gamin ex Ch. Hampton's Poupee D'Or

Ch. Affabulls King of Diamonds....................29
Ch. Vi Du Lac Starhaven's Hot Flash ex Ch. Precious Bulls Copy Girl

Ch. Terrette's Tourbillon D'Gamin CD............29
Ch. Terrette's Chef D'Oeuvre Gamin ex Ch. Hampton's Petite Cherie

Ch. Day Star's Aires of Avlis Bloa................28
Ch. Buntins Bossy Doctor Mark ex Charming Maya Avlis and Bloa

Ch. McBeth's Thunder LeBulRosewood.....................27
Ch. Rosewood Oscar Le Beau ex Ch. Sonlit Europa

Ch. Cox's Goodtime Make His Mark.............26
Ch. Cox's Goodtime Dandy Andy ex Ch. Cox's Goodtime Mindy Lou of K 'n D

Ch. Jackpot! Ez Come…Ez Go.....................26
Ch. Cox's Goodtime Charlie Brown ex Ch. Jackpot! Kwik Pik Tiket Petty

Ch. Terrette's Tourbillon Orage....................26
Ch. Terrette's Tourbillon D'Gamin ex Regina De Cro Marin

Ch. Adams King of the Road.........................25
Ch. Balihai's Quad ex Ch. Adams Lucky Lady

Ch. Cox's Goodtime Ace In The Hole..............25
Ch. Adams Unique Physique ex Ch. Cox's Goodtime Dorene

Ch. Here Tis'Up'N'Adam de McKee...............24
Ch. L'Cream Dream Machine D'McKee ex Ch. La Petite Charomix DeMcKee

Ch. Taurustrail Fearless................................24
Ch. Balihai's Quad ex Ch. Adams Hot Stuff

Ch. Enstrom's El Bee Great..........................23
Ch. Enstrom's Will He Make It ex Ch. Enstrom's Puddin's Princess

Ch. Fairmont's Heart to Beat........................23
Ch. Jimmy Lee's Sparkle ex Ch. Jimmy Lee's Bandolero of Ono

Ch. H and A's Top Hat and Tails...................23
Ch. Fairmont's Radar Ahead ex Ch. Cox's Goodtime Little Bit

Ch. Tidewater's Monte Carlo Jackpot...........23
Ch. Jackpot! Sir Winzalot of Tidewater ex Ch. Tidewaters Hurricane Allis

Ch. Cox's Goodtime Barnstormer.................22
Ch. Cox's Goodtime The Jock ex Cox's Goodtime Jubilee

Ch. Cox's Goodtime Bit O'Gold.....................22
Ch. Cox's Goodtime Dandy Andy ex Ch. Cox's Goodtime Meagan of Ace

Ch. Cox's Goodtime Polar Bear.....................22
Ch. Cox's Goodtime Jack of Jock ex Ch. Cox's Goodtime Isabella

Ch Jackpot! Money Money Money................22
Ch. Cox's Goodtime Barnstormer ex Ch. Jackpot! Diva La Vegas

Ch. Twin Lakes EZ Rider...............................22
Ch. Jackpot! EZ Come…EZ Go ex Ch. Twin Lakes She's A Lulu

APPENDIX II
Top-Producing Bitches

Every effort has been made to ensure the accuracy of these records, but an occasional error or omission may have crept in and we apologize for that. The records, as recorded and published by the American Kennel Club and published in the books by Camino Books, Inc., are as follows for top-producing bitches through February 2006:

Ch. Mademoiselle Eve 14
Ch. Fairmont's Radar Ahead ex Ch. Fairmont's Good Time Minnie

Ch. Apogee's Honey Jo Woody 11
Ch. Apogee's Making The Bacon ex Ch. El Bee Great

Ch. McBeth's Lizz Taylor 11
Ch. McBeth's Thunder LeBulRosewood ex Ch. H and A's Fleur D'Amour

Ch. Bon Marv's Glory 10
Ch. Adams King of the Road ex Ch. Cox's Goodtime Lou Annie

Ch. Schmidt's Madame Patachou 10
Ch. Ullah's Charmeur ex Ch. Hampton's Jolie Coquette

Ch. Wolf N Wrinkles Merryheart 10
Ch. Billet Doux Faberge ex Ch. Collom's Petite Sherrie

Ch. Cox's Goodtime Meagan of Ace 9
Ch. Cox's Goodtime Ace In The Hole ex Cox's Goodtime Sugar Plum

Ch. Cox's Goodtime Mindy Lou Of K 'n D 9
K & D Hombre un De Radar ex Ch. Mademoiselle Eve

Ch. Enstrom's Puddin's Princess 9
Ch. Major Golden Nugget ex Ch. Enstrom's Vanilla Puddin

Ch. Fabelhaft Flower Power 9
Ch. Eltorro's Roch Voisine ex Ch. Firesides Snow Belle

Ch. Jaguar's Desiree of Bandog 9
Ch. Jaguar's Bon Vivante ex Jaguar's Shirley

Ch. La Petite Bijou de Rire 9
Buster Brown's Amos ex Ch. Ms Molly's Precious Moments

Ch. Legacy Ms Behavin O'Rosewood 9
Ch. Rosewood Oscar LeBeau ex Ch. Tambo's Dahlia

Manilee Raisin Cane Flare Path 9
Flarepath Golden Boy Manilee ex Flarepath Chole

Ch. Neblon Pudgybull D'Hedgebrook 9
Ch. Cox's Goodtime Charlie Brown ex Ch. Bon Marv's Glory

Ch. Padlock's I'm Some Bunny 9
Ch. Apogee's Roger Rabbit ex Starhaven Passion At Padlock

APPENDIX III
Winners of the National Specialty

UNDER THE AUSPICES OF THE FRENCH BULL DOG CLUB OF AMERICA
(B = bitch; D = dog)

1898	Dimboolaa (D)	1958	Ch. Ber-Neil's Jeepers Jackie (D)
1910	Ch. Nellcote Gamin (D)	1959	Ch. Ber-Neil's Jeepers Jackie (D)
1911	Ch. Pourquoi Pas (D)	1960	Ch. Ber-Neil's Jeepers Jackie (D)
1912	Ch. Gamin's Riquet (D)	1961	Ch. Ber-Neil's Jeepers Jackie (D)
1913	Denault's Gamin (D)	1962	Ch. Laurelwood Cream Puff (B)
1914	Dr. Deluxe (D)	1963	Ch. Emilie's Bonne Ami Tanya (B)
1915	Ch. Gamin's Rival (D)	1964	Ch. Petit Pierrot de Savage (D)
1916	Ch. Young's Pourquoi Pas (D)	1965	Ch. Pierrot of Quatt (D)
1917	Ch. Gamin's Rival Jr. (D)	1966	Ch. Ralanda Ami Michelle (B)
1918	Monte Carlo Mona Lisa (B)	1967	Ch. Ralanda Ami Hollee (B)
1919	Ch. La Reine d'Anjou (B)	1968	Ch. Chaseholme Mr. Chips (D)
1920	LaFrance Model II (D)	1969	Ch. Terrette's Tourbillon D'Gamin CD (D)
1921	LaFrance Model II (D)	1970	Ch. Chaseholme Mr. Chips (D)
1922	La Fleur d'Anjou (B)	1971	Ch. Chaseholme Mr. Chips (D)
1923	La Fleur d'Anjou (B)	1972	Ch. Hampton's Charlemagne (D)
1924	Evergay Charmer (B)	1973	Ch. Jimmy Lee's Flip (D)
1925	Ch. Denault's Parsque (D)	1974	Ch. Hampton's Charlemagne (D)
1926	Ch. Evergay Charmer (B)	1975	Ch. Hover's Snow White (B)
1927	Franc (D)	1976	Ch. Lavander's Liqueur de Fleur (B)
1928	Denault's Navina (B)	1977	Ch. Les Britan Forbidden Apple (D)
1929	Jeff III (D)	1978	Ch. Les Britan Forbidden Apple (D)
1930	Nelz Lisette of Pinetum (B)	1979	Ch. Hover's Annabella d'Or (B)
1931	Ch. Charmeuse d'Amourette (B)	1980	Ch. Fran Mar Dude d'Angel (D)
1932	Ch. Charmeuse d'Amourette (B)	1981	Ch. Heaton's Henry (D)
1933	Ch. Haworth Phoebus (D)	1982	Ch. D'zongs Firecracker (D)
1934	Nelz Ambeau of Pinetum (D)	1983	Adams' Pride n Joie de Le Fox (B)
1935	LaFrance Model III (D)	1984	Ch. Jaguar's Creme de la Creme (D)
1936	Ch. LaFrance Model III (D)	1985	Ch. Enstrom's Squatty Body (D)
1937	Miss Modesty (B)	1986	Ch. Wolf N' Wrinkles J. Edgar (D)
1938	Ch. Miss Modesty (B)	1987	Stormcrest ML's A.J. of R.J. (D)
1939	Ch. La France Fleurette (B)	1988	Ch. Fishers Lyric August Chase (D)
1940	Ch. Nap Phoebus (D)	1989	Ch. Player Edward Puck (D)
1941	Boalah Belle of Albeth (B)	1990	Ch. Bandog's Earnin' Respect (D)
1942	Ch. Haworth Bon Michel (D)	1991	Ch. Cox's Goodtime Charlie Brown (D)
1943	Ch. Glamourette (B)	1992	Ch. Bandog's Earnin' Respect (D)
1944	Ch. Glamourette (B)	1993	Ch. Bandog's One In A Million (D)
1945	Ch. Haworth Bon Michel II (D)	1994	Ch. Blazin Bul-Marc-It Marianette (D)
1946	Ch. Dooly's Nanette (B)	1995	Ch. Cox's Goodtime Sundance Kid (D)
1947	Ch. Haworth Bon Michel II (D)	1996	Ch. Bandog's Earnin' Respect (D)
1948	Ch. Haworth Bon Michel II (D)	1997	Ch. Blazin's Ironside Perry of NRW (D)
1949	Ch. Le Petit Marquis de La France II (D)	1998	Ch. Obsession dell Akiris (B)
1950	Ch. Le Petit Marquis de La France II (D)	1999	Ch. Sonlit Willa Steele (B)
1951	Ch. Le Petit Marquis de La France II (D)	2000	Ch. Obsession dell Akiris (B)
1952	Ch. Ackerman's Petit Poupee (B)	2001	Ch. Obsession dell Akiris (B)
1953	Ch. Bouquet Nouvelle Ami (D)	2002	Ch. Bandog's Jump for Joy (B)
1954	Ch. Bouquet Nouvelle Ami (D)	2003	Ch. Jackpot! I'm the Boss of JustUs (D)
1955	Ch. Le Petit Marquis de La France III (D)	2004	Ch. Vancroft LeFox American Boy (D)
1956	Ch. Bouquet Nouvelle Ami (D)	2005	Ch. Shann's Pudgybull Houdini (D)
1957	Ch. Bouquet Nouvelle Ami (D)	2006	Ch. Fabelhaft Too Hot To Handle (D)

APPENDIX IV
Regional French Bulldog Clubs

Established and Developing Clubs

French Bulldog Fanciers of Mid-Florida

Dallas/Ft. Worth French Bulldog Club
www.frenchietales.com

Northern California French Bulldog Club
www.ncfbc.com

Heart of Texas French Bulldog Club
www.hotfrenchbulldogs.com

Southeast French Bulldog Club
www.sefbdc.com

Greater Willamette Valley French Bulldog Club

French Bulldog Fanciers of Southern California
www.frenchiesfirst.com

Central Arizona French Bulldog Club
www.cafbc.com

APPENDIX V
Publications of Interest

BREED BOOKS

Alford, Arlie Amarie, *Celebrating Frenchies*, Mendota, MN: ArDesign, 2003.

Dannel, Kathy, *The French Bulldog: An Owner's Guide to a Happy Healthy Pet*, New York: Howell Book House, 2000.

Eltinge, Steve, *The French Bulldog,* Santa Barbara, CA: MIP Publishing.

French Bull Dog Club of America, *The French Bulldog,* 1926.

French Bull Dog Club of America,*The French Bulldog—Breed Standard Illustrated*, second printing, 2004.

Grebe, Janice, *Healthy Frenchies: An Owner's Manual,* Mendota, MN: ArDesign, 1998.

Grebe, Janice, and Steve Eltinge, *The Flat Face Encyclopedia—Bulldogs and French Bulldogs from A to Z*, Mendota, MN: ArDesign, 1997.

Hickman, Beth, *Featuring Frenchies: A French Bulldog Handbook*, Southwind Press, 1986.

Lee, Muriel, *French Bulldog*, Surrey, England: Interpet Publishing, 2003.

Lee, Muriel, *The French Bulldog: A Complete and Reliable Handbook,* Neptune City, NJ: TFH Publications, 2001.

Nicholas, Anna Katherine, *French Bulldogs*, Neptune City, NJ: TFH Publications, 1989.

Pronek, Neal, *How to Raise and Train a French Bulldog*, Neptune City, NJ: TFH Publications, 1965.

Vitcak, Kathy Dannel, *The French Bulldog International Annual*, 2002.

PEDIGREE REFERENCE BOOKS

French Bulldog Champions, 1952–1988, Nevada: E. E. Camino.

French Bulldog Champions, 1989–2000, Nevada: E. E. Camino.

French Bulldog Champions, 2001–2004, Nevada: E. E. Camino.

PERIODICALS

The French Bull Dog
A beautiful monthly magazine published by the French Bull Dog Club of America that consisted of nine issues published between January 1913 and December 1913. "A magazine devoted to promoting the interest of the French Bulldog throughout the world." Highly collectible and difficult to find.

The French Bullytin
Arlie Amarie Alford (ArDesign), publisher and editor; 1982 to the present.

The Frenchie Fancier
Quarterly publication by the Dockstaders; 36 issues between 1974 and 1979. Difficult to find and the only breed magazine since 1913.

Just Frenchies
Ron and Suzanne Readmond, publishers; Muriel Lee, editor; 2002 to the present.

GENERAL SITES

American Kennel Club
www.akc.org
Fédération Cynologique Internationale
www.fci.be
The Kennel Club
www.thekennelclub.org.uk

HEALTH SITES

Canine Health Foundation
www.ackchf.org
Orthopedic Foundation for Animals (OFA)
www.offa.org
Canine Health Information Center (CHIC)
www.caninehealthinfo.org
Brachycephalic Breeds
www.frogdog.org/flat_faced

RESCUE

French Bulldog Rescue Network
www.frenchbulldogrescue.org
French Bulldog Connection Rescue
www.frenchbulldogconnection.org

THERAPY

The Bright and Beautiful Therapy Dogs
www.pet-therapist.com
Therapy Dogs International
www.tdi-dog.org
Delta Society
www.deltasociety.org

ART

William Secord Gallery
www.dogpainting.com

FRENCH BULLDOG CLUBS AROUND THE WORLD

Austria
Österreichischen Club für Französische Bulldoggen
www.franzbull.at

Australia
The French Bulldog Club of Victoria
www.geocities.com/fbcvau

Belgium
De Koninklijke Belgische Klub van de Franse Bulldog
www.belgianfrenchbulldogclub.be

Canada
The French Bulldog Fanciers of Canada
www.frenchbulldogfanciers.com

Czech Republic
Klub Francouzských buldocků Praha
http://kfb.praha.sweb.cz

Denmark
Bulldog-Klubben
www.bulldogklubben.dk

Finland
SuomenRanskanbulldogit ry
www.toydogs.net/rb

France
Le Club du Bouledogue Français
www.cbf-asso.org

Germany
Internationaler Klub für Französische Bulldoggen e.V.
www.ikfb.de

Netherlands
Hollandse Bulldoggen Club
www.hbc-fransebulldog.nl

New Zealand
Southern Bulldog Club
http://bulldogz.com/sbc

Norway
Norsk Bulldog Klubb
www.norskbulldogklubb.net

Poland
Klub Buldoga Francuskiego W Polsce
http://klub.100pociech.com

Russia
French Bulldog Club Russia
www.frenchbulldog.ru

Spain
El Club Español de Amigos del Bulldog Francés
www.bulldog-frances.com

Sweden
Fransk Bulldogg Klub Sverige
http://fbksverige.se

Switzerland
Schweizerischer Klub für Französische Bulldoggen
www.suisse-bully.ch

United Kingdom
French Bulldog Club of England
www.frenchbulldogclubofengland.org

United States of America
French Bull Dog Club of America
www.frenchbulldogclub.org

INDEX

Page numbers in bold denote illustrations.